Mediterranean
Kitchen Garden

Mediterranean Kitchen Garden

by Mariano Bueno
Translated and edited by Evelyn FitzHerbert

F

FRANCES LINCOLN LIMITED
PUBLISHERS

Frances Lincoln Limited
4 Torriano Mews
Torriano Avenue
London NW5 2RZ
www.franceslincoln.com

Mediterranean Kitchen Garden
Copyright © Frances Lincoln Limited 2010
Text copyright © Mariano Bueno 2010
For copyright in the illustrations see page 160

First Frances Lincoln edition 2010

A catalogue record for this book is available from the
British Library.

ISBN 978 0 7112 3064 4
Printed and bound in China
1 2 3 4 5 6 7 8 9

Contents

PREFACE
Mary Keen

Several years ago, when I had a commission to redesign and plan a vegetable garden in Greece, I searched for a book on the subject. There seemed to be nothing on offer. I failed to find anything at the Royal Horticultural Society library, or on line, either about the Mediterranean or about California, which has a similar climate. A kind friend with a house in Greece copied out some pages of the odd magazine for me, and when I happened to be in Italy I bought a picture book called *Il Mio Orto* and stumbled through it, but I was still not much the wiser.

The Greeks who grew vegetables for my clients, using improbably antique implements, tried to communicate their old world techniques, but there was a language problem and my skills were so different from theirs. There was much flooding of vegetables and very little hoeing, and in hot summers there was an embarrassing lack of choice for a succession of exasperated chefs, who called for raspberries and pears. I wish this book had been around when I needed it, but I am delighted that such an authoritative volume can now save other gardeners from the trials and errors that were my initiation to kitchen gardening far from the temperate climate of home.

For those who think that they will never grow vegetables abroad, it is worth saying that the book is not restricted to Mediterranean gardeners and has a lot to teach anyone who wants to grow their own produce organically in any climate. Mariano Bueno is Spain's top organic gardener. I learned plenty of techniques that will be useful in the British Isles as well as in Greece. In hot summers, the drip irrigation recommended in the book, rather than the flooding I saw practised by the Greek gardeners, would be practical and eco-friendly. Mulching and shade netting may be useful tricks in dry summers. A long chapter on orchards is as good on apples and pears as it is on oranges and lemons. It would have been ideal information for me to give

the chefs who could not believe that pomegranates would just have to do instead of pears. I now have a much better idea of what temperatures are suitable for different fruits, and pears were never going to be on the menu in Corfu. I know too that nasturtiums will look ravishing under orange trees, as there is a picture to rival Monet's garden showing exactly that.

Basic principles are explained clearly, and encouragement is a great feature of this book. Anyone trying productive growing for the first time might be captivated by a section headed 'The instant garden'. This explains a simple form of permaculture and no-dig principles, so that the author can exclaim with conviction 'Take heart, all you lazy people out there: plentiful harvests await you!' But this is by no means a book solely for the beginner. For the more experienced, there are plenty of tips. I did not know that pine needles, being acid, make a good mulch for strawberries, nor that if you introduce earwigs to your artichokes you will solve the blackfly problem. There are very practical and specific instructions for compost-making and for sharpening secateurs while keeping the blade in oil, as well as for watering tomatoes.

I like the author's approach and light touch. He gives advice on working with the moon. Admitting that while some may deny the existence of lunar influences and others may practise blind faith, he writes 'Perhaps the best course is to be open-minded and willing to experiment.'

The book gives one the impression of wise counsel tactfully offered by someone who has gardened methodically for years. And the publisher has been clever to find a translator whose writing is as fresh as the produce pictured on the pages of the book. Evelyn FitzHerbert is Evelyn Waugh's granddaughter and clearly she has, like many of the Waugh family, inherited a particular talent for writing.

INTRODUCTION

A small plot of earth, where you can connect with nature, the seasons and the abundance of the land, makes an invaluable contribution to the quality of life. Whether you have a large kitchen garden or a tiny patch, tending your garden will bring you great happiness, as you dig, sow, weed, harvest or simply stroll through it, observing every corner, plant and flower.

There is no better way to ensure a healthy diet for yourself and your family than by growing your own fruit, vegetables and culinary herbs. It need not stop there: you can also grow a wide range of medicinal plants with which to make simple remedies for common minor ailments, as well as vitalizing sprays for your garden plants.

This book goes further than that and teaches you how to apply organic principles to your gardening, so that you can give something back to the soil. There is no need to use chemical fertilizers, insecticides or herbicides to grow your tomatoes and lettuces. Gardening can be done perfectly well using natural methods and substances that respect your health and that of your environment. You will improve soil fertility at the same time as enjoying healthy, vigorous plants and plentiful harvests.

With this practical gardening book I hope you will enjoy as much as I have the pleasures of growing healthy plants and eating succulent fresh fruit and vegetables. My greatest wish is that every day you delight a little more in your garden, in the beautiful spaces you have created, and in your life.

MAKING A KITCHEN GARDEN

THE SPACE

It is usually reckoned that it takes about 250m²/300yd² of land to produce all the vegetables for one person on a daily basis – so a family of four wishing to be totally self-sufficient in vegetables might need around 1000m²/1200yd². However, you can grow enough vegetables to make a significant contribution to your family's diet in a space much smaller than that. Even if you only have a terrace you will find that it is possible to grow a large variety of vegetables, as well as many aromatic and medicinal plants. If you have a good-sized garden you can also consider planting fruit trees, preferably along the edges or grouped together in an orchard. With a smaller plot it is best to restrict yourself to growing vegetables, as within a few years the shade cast by trees and their avid take-up of nutrients will make vegetable gardening impossible.

Light and orientation

It is important that a vegetable garden receives several hours of sunlight each day. Plants need solar radiation to photosynthesize, and their development and nutrient and vitamin content are dependent on it.

Some plants, such as those of the solanaceae family (including tomatoes, peppers and aubergines/eggplants) and cucurbits (melons, cucumbers, courgettes/zucchini, etc.), need a lot of light and heat. Others, such as escarole (broad-leaved endive), Swiss chard, cabbage and spinach, will grow well with less.

Water

Too much water causes rotting and makes plants susceptible to parasitic fungi. Lack of water slows down vegetative development and turns the plants fibrous and hard with a tendency to bolt and flower. How the garden is to be irrigated must be considered when planning the layout of beds.

A layout of beds and paths in a sunny garden.

GARDEN DESIGN

Plant salad crops in succession for a regular supply.

The first step in creating a garden is to come up with a design that incorporates all the space available. This will help to maximize the use of the space and get the best results for the least effort.

What would you like to eat?

Planning what to grow is as important as a good design. For this you need to consider your local climate (see page 18) and think about what you eat. There is little point in planting twenty cabbages if you don't like cabbage. On the other hand, if you eat salad every day, it makes sense to sow and plant lettuces on a regular basis: planting fifteen or twenty lettuces every two weeks or once a month makes for a staggered supply and means you never go without. As for courgettes (zucchini), unless you want to be giving them away by the kilo three or four plants will provide plenty for a family´s needs.

Planning

As a garden is constantly evolving, a map or sketch showing the distribution of the beds and spaces is very useful. It is important to date your plans and number or letter the beds and even the rows in the beds. Although this might seem an onerous task, it is the only way to plan crop rotation (see page 45) over the years.

Some plants have longer growing cycles than others, so it is a good idea to make a plan for every season of the year or at least for every two seasons, e.g. spring/summer and autumn/winter.

GARDEN LAYOUT

There are many different ways of working and preparing the soil for a garden. The traditional method in many Mediterranean countries is to make a system of beds which are irrigated by water circulated by means of small channels or ditches. This method, known as flood irrigation, is very labour intensive. The soil is compacted by the water and needs endless tilling, and the high evaporation caused by the soil's exposure to the sun makes for profligate use of water, especially in high summer. In addition, the beds need constant weeding, as the flooding makes a weed-suppressing straw mulch impractical.

Far preferable is a system of beds with drip irrigation. The advantages of this method are that the soil is kept constantly watered and the irrigation can be controlled electronically. An electronic program opens and closes the water supply according to the climatic conditions. This both saves water and allows you to be absent for long periods without losing all your crops for lack of watering. It also makes it possible to use a mulch of straw (or other organic matter), which, besides saving water by lessening evaporation from the soil, saves you having to weed, as weeds do not grow in the shade produced by the mulch. Finally, it makes it possible to cultivate a flat or gently sloped piece of land without having to remake beds and ditches every time you irrigate in order to get the water circulating where needed. If a drip irrigation system seems more elaborate than the size of your garden calls for, you can water with a garden hosepipe perfectly satisfactorily.

So why make beds at all? Beds have many functions, the most important of which are to limit the space under cultivation and, by demarcating paths, avoid the compaction of the soil where plants will be cultivated. The beds need to stay as aerated as possible, as compacted earth reduces the root development of plants and makes it difficult for worms, bacteria and micro-organisms to do the work that is essential for a fertile living soil.

What kind of bed?

What type of bed is suitable depends on the garden, the soil, the climate and the plants to be grown. Two types of beds are illustrated in the following pages: raised beds and level beds, the latter using the method of the Majorcan gardener Gaspar Caballero. Either type is preferable to sunken beds.

Level beds – beds at the same level as the ground – are easy to make and good in hot climates and dry conditions, as with less surface exposed to the air and sun there is much less evaporation than there is with raised beds.

Raised beds are good for temperate climates and ideal for humid regions, where the problem is not lack of water but too much of it, and level beds might suffer from flooding. Another advantage of raised beds is that they are much less laborious to work: less bending is necessary, as you can work them while adopting a fairly comfortable posture.

Making raised beds

Raised beds are some 120cm/4ft wide and 30–50cm/12–20in high (or higher in wet areas), with paths between 50–60cm/20–24in wide. The beds should be no longer than 6m/20ft; 4m/13ft is a good manageable length. Make them as follows (as illustrated on page 16):

1   Dig the ground where the beds are to go, as deep as possible. You can spread compost on the ground before digging, so that it mixes in with the soil, but it is better to lay compost on the surface after digging, without mixing it in. Mark out the beds, not more than 120cm/4ft wide and between 4m/13ft and 6m/20ft long. Leave paths at least 50cm/20in wide between the beds. Using a spade, heap the soil from the paths on to the beds, giving these a height of some 25–50cm/10–20in.

2   Give the beds form and rake them to remove stones and hard compacted lumps, depositing these on the paths. The top of the bed should now be some 105–110cm/3½ft wide.

3   Spread 2–4cm/¾–1½in of compost on the beds.

4   On top lay porous pipes or drip irrigation tubes with holes every 33cm/12in. The beds are now ready for use.

5 When planting, aim to have the roots of the plants close to the drip holes.

6 Mulching the beds with straw will avoid excessive evaporation and impede the growth of weeds.

Making level beds

The level beds used by Gaspar Caballero are 150cm/5ft wide, with stones or bricks spaced along the centre of each bed to make it possible to work the beds without stepping on them. Make them as follows (as illustrated on page 17):

1 Using sticks and string, mark out beds, each 150m/5ft wide and no longer than 6m/20ft. Leave paths 50–70cm/20–27in wide between them.

2 Dig the beds to a depth of 25–40cm/10–16in. With a rake, level the soil and remove stones and lumps. With string, mark out a central strip 30cm/12in wide and 60cm/24in from either edge of the bed.

3 Lay big flat stones or bricks spaced 60cm/24in apart along this central strip.

4 Between the stones plant aromatic, ornamental or medicinal plants. Spread compost 2–4cm/¾–1½in deep on the two sides of each bed, avoiding stepping on the area to be planted.

5 Lay porous pipes or drip irrigation tubes in parallel lines along the beds.

6 The beds are now ready for planting. Mulch with straw as for raised beds.

Using the beds

While making beds might appear a lot of work initially, it is a task that has to be done only once. To plant a new crop, simply remove the mulch, add more compost and plant; then return the mulch around the new plants. If sowing green (string or flat pole) beans, peas, broad (fava) beans, or root crops such as onions, leeks and garlic, it is not even necessary to add compost. When sowing seed, as opposed to planting, don't put back the mulch until the seeds have germinated and the seedlings are visible. The only occasion when you need to work the soil is when heavy rain has compacted ground not covered by mulch. Even then it is only necessary to loosen the earth using a double-handled fork or *grenillette*.

Sowing a green manure every three or four years, or in beds that are lying empty, will improve the structure of the soil. These plants, such as vetch or field beans, improve the soil deep down as well as fertilizing it in a natural way.

Raised bed.

Level bed.

Making raised beds

1 Dig the ground and mark out the beds.

2 Give the beds form and remove stones and lumps.

3 Spread compost.

4 Lay out porous pipes or drip irrigation tubes.

5 Plant close to drip holes.

6 Mulch with straw.

Making level beds

1 Mark out the beds.

2 Dig the beds and mark out a central strip.

3 Lay flat stones along the central strip.

4 Plant aromatic or ornamental plants between the stones.

5 Lay porous pipes or drip irrigation tubes on the beds.

6 The planted beds.

CLIMATE

The climate, with its constant variations and changes, is the most important of all the environmental factors affecting plant life. For farmers it has always been a major preoccupation. The forecast of rain, summer heat, strong autumn winds or intense cold and freezing in winter is what mainly determines gardening tasks and planting. The climatic conditions of the region, together with the local microclimate (see below) and the specific location of the garden, are the guiding factors in terms of when to sow and transplant outside. They also limit the growth of some plants and the harvest that can be expected.

Knowing local climatic conditions and being able to forecast roughly when rain, cold or heat are coming

also help to anticipate favourable conditions for pest infestations. Plagues of aphids or mites or diseases such as downy and powdery mildew can be avoided or mitigated by putting in place protective measures or by reinforcing plants with vitalizing plant preparations.

However, planning what you do is no easy task given the numerous variables involved. Also, apart from the fact that the weather from one year to the next can be unpredictable, microclimatic factors are critical.

Plants and climate

Temperature and humidity are environmental factors that impose clear limits on what you can cultivate. Every plant is adapted to the temperatures and ambient humidity of its place of origin. It is also adapted to a particular sequence of heat and cold. Although it will have a degree of tolerance, the bigger the difference in such factors between the plant's place of origin and where it is now being cultivated, the more problems it is likely to have in completing its life cycle.

The dates of the last and first frosts are important (see opposite), as they mark the beginning and end of the cultivation of many vegetables and annual herbaceous plants. It is, however, possible to extend the growing season with protection and the creation of microclimates.

Maximum and minimum temperatures also need to be borne in mind. Each plant has its limits in terms of resistance at specific altitudes. When choosing perennial plants, this may be a limiting factor.

Hours of sunshine

A map showing average annual hours of sunshine is helpful when you are deciding whether to cultivate certain plants. There are a number of plants that need long periods of exposure to light to grow well and produce fruit: such plants include tomatoes, aubergines (eggplants), melons and cucumbers. Insufficient hours of sunlight or a sharp fall in temperature at nightfall can be enough to stunt their normal development.

Climatic maps

A climate map is useful when planning a garden. Unfortunately those available give data only for large

Microclimates

- A garden's orography and solar exposure determine specific microclimates.
- A mountain creates a different microclimate on each slope, on the summit and in the valley at its side. The mountain can channel air, producing wind that dries out the soil and makes cultivation of delicate plants impossible.
- Coastal zones and lowland river plains have a milder climate than inland regions. This is due to the moderating effect that big masses of water (seas, rivers, reservoirs, lakes) have on thermal contrasts in the surrounding area. There is less heat in summer, less cold in winter and a gentler transition between the two.
- Forests regulate the amount and speed of rain water reaching the ground and also moderate the speed of winds and the temperature changes through the day.
- Cities also provide microclimates that are stable and favourable for gardening. The density of buildings and the absorbing thermal effect of asphalt on the whole result in a higher average temperature than elsewhere.
- Hedges moderate temperatures, wind strength and humidity.

areas such as a province. The ideal solution is to systematically collect data in order to make a climate profile of your area, based on all the microclimates that come together there. Some town halls regularly publish climate data relating to the town.

Climate zones

A climate zone map is helpful in giving a general idea of a region´s climate, but it is important to bear in mind local variations and microclimates.

- **Temperate zones – Mediterranean climate**
  These have fairly stable climates. Winters are mild and it rarely freezes; summers, while hot, are not suffocating.
- **Cold-temperate zones – oceanic climate**
  These benefit from the ocean´s mitigating effect on temperature extremes. The effect of a large mass of water is to take the edge off winter cold and alleviate summer heat.
- **Cold zones – mountain climate**
  Above a certain altitude average temperatures are usually low, despite days often being sunny. This is due to air being colder higher up.
- **Hot zones – desert or steppe climates**
  These regions are normally free from cold periods and nightly frosts, but they have the disadvantage of being extremely hot and dry for most of the year.
- **Zones of contrast – continental climate**
  These have very cold winters and very hot summers. They are often regions of great plains, suitable for pasture and growing cereals. Garden plants adapt well in such regions, though they can be weakened by the extreme temperatures that they have to tolerate in summer and winter.

Last and first frosts

The date of the last winter/spring frost of the year is what determines when you can safely sow and plant out plants sensitive to cold. It is tempting to think that the earlier you sow or plant, the earlier you will harvest; however, premature sowing or transplanting is risky and your best efforts can be wrecked overnight. So it is best to wait until the likely date of the last frost has passed. A simple and effective way of judging this is to plant a hawthorn bush in your garden and keep an eye on it. This clever plant, wherever it may be growing, waits until all risk of frost is over before it flowers.

Autumn/winter frosts mark the end of the season when sensitive plants such as tomatoes, aubergines, peppers and green beans can be left outside. They also signal the end of potential harvests.

It is recommended that every gardener should make a note of the exact dates of first and last frosts in their locality, in order to establish a better approximation over a period of time.

Frosts

- The worst frosts are the early and late ones, which catch plants off-guard.
- A gentle cold wind that dies down when it gets dark on clear nights is a possible indicator of frost.
- There is more likelihood of late frosts in dry springs than in wet ones.
- Herbaceous plants are more susceptible to frost damage than woody plants. Evergreens suffer from cold more than deciduous plants.
- Frosts are more common in sandy soils than in clay soils.
- It is worth paying attention to weather forecasts and any clues in your environment, as there are always precautionary measures that can be taken to mitigate the effects of frost.

The hawthorn will not flower until all risk of frost is past.

TOOLS

There are two distinct phases of work in the garden.

Construction

The most laborious stages are digging and preparing the soil for the first time, and making the beds. A good sturdy mattock is perhaps essential for working the earth to a decent depth, and getting rid of roots and rocks. A powerful cultivator or rotovator can also save work for large areas. It is not necessary to buy one: you can be rent one by the day or contract a gardener to do the work.

Once the beds and the basic structure of the garden are in place, no big machines or complicated tools will be needed, unless you remodel the garden.

Maintenance

Few tools are needed for general maintenance. Earthworms will keep the soil aerated if you do not tread on the soil and keep it damp with a permanent mulch. For many tasks, hands will suffice and give you more contact with nature – indeed life itself.

Basic tools

- Mattock for preparing beds
- Spade, transplanting trowel and hoe for superficial digging
- Strong leather gloves for working with thorny plants
- A springbok rake for raking up leaves where they are a nuisance
- A rake for removing stones, levelling the soil and producing a tilth
- A double-handled fork – this facilitates moving the earth deep down without turning it

Pruning tools

- Secateurs – sturdy and with a good spring
- Long-handled secateurs with a double lock system in two positions for average to thicker branches
- A saw with a samurai system of sharpening

Tips for tools

- If you do not have a shredder for cutting up prunings and other woody remains, you can go over fallen leaves and prunings with a lawn mower. This cuts the remains into smaller pieces that can then be fed to the compost heap. The smaller the pieces, the faster the composting process; adding carbon-rich material such as this achieves a perfect nitrogen/carbon balance and a good texture.
- When choosing tools, usefulness should take precedence but also pay attention to comfort (look for long ergonomic handles).
- To sharpen secateurs, submerge the blades in oil and sharpen, respecting the bevelled edge. Disinfect with 90 per cent alcohol and use sandpaper to get rid of rust.

Machine tools

- A strimmer with a head that takes nylon twine for clearing paths and between fruit trees
- A shredder for shredding pruning remains and larger vegetable trimmings

Rotovating.

Using a double-handled fork to dig potatoes.

Raking.

Hoeing.

Breaking soil up with a mattock.

SOIL

Soil texture, structure and pH

The soil in which plants take root and grow is complex, combining minerals, organic matter in varying states of decomposition and millions of micro- and macro-organisms. All these together confer special qualities on the soil and make the development of life possible. The interaction of the different elements provides the soil with its texture, which is related to the proportion of clay, sand and organic matter. Another aspect is the structure of the soil, which is determined by the size of the crumbs made when the particles combine and the size of the spaces between them.

The pH represents the alkalinity or acidity of the soil. The ideal pH for plant development lies between 5.5 and 7, and this is also favourable for the activity of micro-organisms. The ideal is to have maximum biodiversity, so that the soil is able to be a living ecosystem. For this the numerous communities of micro-organisms are important.

Soil is usually classified into three basic categories, according to which size of particle dominates: sand (light), loam (balanced) and clay (heavy).

Sandy soils are very light and easy to work. However, they allow water, and with it nutrients, to drain away quickly and thus need nutrient addition and assiduous watering. They can be improved by the addition of a lot of compost and if possible clay soil.

A loam is a balanced mix of clay soil, sandy soil, silt (similar to clay) and humus. It is the ideal soil for a garden, as it is easy to dig and retains humidity well without losing its sponginess.

Clay soils are compacted by rain or watering and when dry can become brick hard, making them difficult to dig. It helps to add sandy soil and porous sands such as perlite, coconut fibre or other spongy material. Compost added to heavy soils needs to be well broken down to avoid anaerobic fermentation.

Feeding the garden

Chemical synthetic fertilizers are not used in organic agriculture. Instead compost, permanent mulch with organic matter (see page 43) and green manures (see pages 15 and 46) are more than sufficient to give plants the nutrients they need.

In organic gardening feeding the soil is more important than feeding the plants. Plants do not have digestive systems. Instead, the host of bacteria, fungi, worms and other micro-organisms living in the earth break down the nutrients into a form available to the plants.

To maintain and increase the soil's fertility, you need to incorporate organic material into the soil on a regular basis. Already decomposed matter – compost, manure – is suitable. Although it is possible to buy compost, making your own from your domestic waste is satisfying and also interesting, as described on the following pages.

Digging

Digging puts soil into contact with air and increases the activity of micro-organisms. In nature and in the no-dig method, where compost is applied on top of the soil and covered with a mulch, the aeration of the soil is achieved by earthworms with their endless tunnelling. Aeration is essential to avoid the fermentation of organic matter, which can be harmful to the development of plants. The life of the soil originates mainly in the top 15–25cm/5–10in, which is the warmest and most aerated layer. This is the fertile topsoil and care must be taken while digging not to bury it deeper, where only anaerobic bacteria can thrive.

COMPOST

The addition of compost to a garden is a controversial subject. Some promote adding large quantities of compost (by which is understood manure or other decomposed organic matter), while others say that there is no need and put their trust in the earth's capacity to fertilize itself.

The majority of plants grown for food are very demanding of nutrients. They evolved over the years from wild plants and through selection became big and juicy. Almost all plants now cultivated in gardens are the result of continuous and abundant additions of organic matter and water. This is in stark contrast to the precarious existence of their wild ancestors with much less at their disposal. As a defence mechanism wild plants tend to be bitter and more fibrous, unpalatable to most people. Thus there is little choice but to provide your garden plants regularly with water and organic matter.

Observing and copying nature

Organic matter should be seen as the key to soil fertility and the development of life. Yet it has been systematically despised and ignored. Forgotten and unappreciated, it has been destroyed in incinerators and dumped in landfill sites with non-organic waste.

In nature, plant development is a continuous cycle, thanks to the return of nutrients to the earth. Leaves, plants and dead trees decompose on the ground, leaving a layer of organic composites. These filter nutrients through to the soil and provide food to the plants growing there. Plants eaten by animals are returned to the soil in the form of manure. When animals die they decompose, also providing food to plants. The loss of nutrients through being washed out by rain and filtration down to deeper layers is compensated for by photosynthesis and atmospheric contribution.

All plants, from grasses to large trees, absorb many of the nutrients they use for growth from the air (more than 50 per cent of dehydrated plant matter is carbon). They do this by means of photosynthesis in the leaf 'laboratory', with the energy supplied by solar radiation. Carbon, nitrogen, hydrogen and oxygen – key elements in plant development – are present in the air in large quantities. Thus it is easy to understand how vegetation in woods and forests can grow without needing additional contributions of organic matter.

How much compost?

The amount of compost needed and how old it needs to be depend on the type of plant. Some plants, such as tomatoes, potatoes and artichokes, need a lot of semi-rotted organic matter. At the other extreme are plants such as carrots and green beans that tolerate only very mature compost.

Rotating the crops (see page 45) in the beds enables the most efficient use of the compost. For example, after tomatoes that have been grown with the addition of a large quantity of compost lettuces can be planted in the same place without any more being added. Once the lettuces are harvested, carrots, peas or any leguminous plant can be sown, since these will make maximum use of any organic matter remaining. Once these are harvested, more compost can be added and the cycle can begin again with demanding plants such as courgettes (zucchini), peppers, aubergines (eggplants), etc.

The fertility cycle

The cycle of nutrients returning to the soil is normally broken in agriculture. Harvested vegetables are transported far away, many of them ending up in landfill sites or being incinerated. The nutrient cycle, essential for a fertile soil´s equilibrium, is broken and the atmospheric contribution is hard pressed to compensate for the constant losses.

It should be borne in mind that the soil´s vitality and fertility are more closely connected to the life the soil hosts than to the quantity of minerals it contains. Humus is what provides life to the soil, and humus is the final result of the complex process undergone by organic matter in decomposition. This process is aided by microbiotic and enzyme activity and the inestimable work of earthworms – true workers of the earth, since their labour converts organic matter and minerals into elements that can be assimilated by plants.

Compost

Composting is the natural process by which organic matter breaks down. When something starts to decompose, it is likely to be thrown away without a thought for the hive of activity that it has begun to house. This intense activity of millions of beings is incredibly ordered and sequential, despite the apparent chaos. With the speed of a short lifespan, monstrous microscopic forms and unsuspected ways of life reproduce, preying on each other and feeding through truly miraculous molecular and atomic transformations.

This humble and overlooked process is the keystone of life on this planet. Without it, all the disposable nutrients would stay trapped in complex structures; plants and all who feed on them would die. Composting garden remains and other organic matter and laying the compost they become on the surface of the soil reintroduces them to the nutrient cycle. Compost is without doubt the basis for the correct fertilizing of the soil and one of the main pillars of organic agriculture.

Composting methods

There are three basic methods: composting on the surface, in a heap or in a container (cold composting). Each method has its advantages and disadvantages; the choice will depend on the particular garden in question.

In surface composting the organic matter is spread on the surface. This method increases the soil´s fertility and vitality and works well in damp climates. In hot climates there is a danger that unless the compost is watered the process slows down too much. The compost should be covered with a straw mulch (see page 43) or other organic matter to stop ultraviolet solar radiation from destroying the essential bacterial activity or drying out the compost to such an extent that the bacteria cannot work.

Experience has shown that the traditional method of mixing compost or manure in with the topsoil is actually counterproductive for the majority of crops. Putting decomposing organic matter next to the plant´s roots alters the bacterial balance in the earth. It generates substances toxic to the roots and creates conditions favourable to plagues of damaging pests. It is preferable to put compost on the surface.

When you are composting in heaps or in a container, the variables involved are easier to control and the process can be optimized. Above all, it makes it possible to have compost for use in seedbeds, fresh or partially decomposed compost for preparing beds and mature compost for applying during the productive phase of the plant or when it is needed to give a boost to a particular plant.

The composting process

Materials These are basically all the organic materials and leftovers from the garden, the kitchen, the chicken coop, etc.

- Some materials have a high nitrogen content – for instance, manure, animal remains, leguminous plants, kitchen scraps, comfrey and lawn cuttings (in order of concentration). Others have a high carbon content – such as wood, sawdust, straw, dead leaves, plant remains and weeds (in order of concentration).
- The carbon–nitrogen ratio is important. At the beginning of the composting process it needs to be approximately 30 parts carbon to 1 part nitrogen. Too much carbon will diminish biological activity, too little and the process will speed up too much.

Carbon is found in abundance in dry, cellulose-rich materials. Nitrogen is found in fresh matter, especially in bird manure and leguminous plants.

- The size of individual components influences the speed of decomposition. Smaller particles have more surface area to come under attack by microorganisms, while bigger particles aid aeration of the heap.
- Additives can balance or enrich the compost – for example, rock dust, natural phosphates, calcareous rock (dolomite), iron sulphate or wood ash.

Community of organisms Bacteria, fungi, protozoa, insects, worms, etc. feed on organic matter and, by breaking it down, generate nutrients for plants. During some phases of decomposition the microorganisms remain in a dormant state; in others they take the lead. They act sequentially, breaking down different components of the waste matter in specific ways. Incorporating fresh or old manure into the heap provides more microorganisms, which act as a catalyst in the fermenting process.

pH PH is the level of acidity or alkalinity. A balanced pH is between 6 and 7. Much deviation from these values will result in a reduction of the microbial population. Excessive acidity can be remedied by the addition of pulverized calcareous rock or wood ash. Too much alkalinity can be remedied by the addition of nitrogen-rich matter.

Temperature Temperature is generated by the activity of microorganisms and in a (hot) heap needs to be maintained between 35 and 65°C/95 and 149°F. High temperatures kill off pathogenic microorganisms, parasites and weed seeds. The higher the temperature, the faster is the rate of decomposition.

Volume The compost heap should be a minimum of 50 x 50 x 50cm/20 x 20 x 20in. Less, and the heap loses heat. With sides wider than 150cm/5ft, air, which is necessary for microbiotic life, has difficulty passing through. Higher than 150cm/5ft and the weight compacts the heap, preventing aeration.

Air Air is essential for micro-organisms to break down organic matter aerobically. Insert coarse materials into the centre of the heap to improve aeration and if necessary turn the heap with a fork.

Composting tips

- Location: this should be protected from wind, shaded in summer and sunny in winter. This is because cold, drying out or the wrong level of humidity can slow down or alter the fermentation process.
- Lunar phases: for starting, turning or removing compost, a full moon is best.
- Additions: adding some old compost or manure enriches the mix and speeds up the composting process. Add water to dry materials and specific pulverized minerals to make up for any deficiencies in the soil. This could be lime to add calcium to the soil and increase the pH or gypsum to improve structure in clay soils.
- Reject diseased plants to avoid the disease spreading (in cold composting).
- Alternate dry material with wet, fine with bulky.

Humidity Optimum humidity for aerobic fermentation is 30–70 per cent. When making a heap, check that it is neither too wet nor too dry. Balance it by adding water or varying the proportion of dry to wet matter. Humidity should be kept constant, so far as possible: too dry hinders the vital work of bacteria, enzymes and micro-organisms, while too wet results in stagnation, asphyxiation and putrefaction through lack of air.

Composting in a heap

When supplies of organic matter are plentiful, build up separate piles of materials according to type; once there is a good volume, build the compost heap in one go. Locate the compost heap in a place sheltered from prevailing winds (these can dry out the heap), and in semi-shade to aid the heating-up of the heap and keep it humid. The heap should be near enough to the house so that it is not too much of a chore taking kitchen remains to it, and near where the compost will be needed. A water supply near by, good access for

Compost heaps with a covering of straw.

Turning and watering the compost heap.

Finished compost.

wheelbarrows or a trailer and space around the heap so as to be able to turn it are also important.

It is best to make the heap on a day when the moon is full or nearly full.

1 Start by laying some 10cm/4in of coarse, bulky matter at the bottom to help air circulation. Above this spread a layer of old compost or manure to act as a fermenting catalyst.

2 Build up the heap, alternating layers of bulky matter such as prunings and sweetcorn stalks with finer material such as dry grass cuttings. Water the heap with each successive layer. Aim to have a balance between carbon-rich and nitrogen-rich materials of 30 to 1. From time to time add a layer of old compost or manure as a leaven. The heap should be no wider and no higher than 150cm/5ft (it can be as long as you want).

3 Once it is finished, the heap can be watered with an activator such as urine or a preparation made with nettles, manure, seaweed or comfrey (see page 153). If there is no roof, cover just the top part with a piece of plastic to prevent too much rain entering. The sides should be left open to allow air circulation. Or cover it with a layer of earth or straw, watering well so that it is not removed by wind.

4 In a few days the temperature of the heap should have risen to 65 or 70°C/149 or 158°F. Thermophilic bacteria will be operative, killing off pathogenic germs and weed seeds. (Beware of higher temperatures. If the compost rises above 70°C/158°F or maintains this temperature for many days in a row, it can lose a lot of its nutritional qualities.)

5 After a couple of weeks the temperature will start to fall. You can reactivate the heap by dismantling and rebuilding it, a process known as 'turning'. Again, water it well.

6 From three months on, the compost will be ready for use as fresh compost. For mature compost, leave it to continue its process for another two or three months. From a year on, it will have become humus and will not improve further. It is best used before this point.

Composting in containers

Composting in a container is suitable when only a small amount of compostable material is available. You can make a container from wood, metal mesh or a recycled plastic drum. It is possible to buy a container with a lid and a door at the bottom that allows the mature compost to be removed.

In containers the composting process happens at the ambient temperature. With a volume of less than $1m^3/35ft^3$ the temperature is unlikely to rise appreciably. The decomposition is achieved mostly by mesophyll bacteria.

When composting in a container, it is important to follow the recommendations for composting in a heap and some additional ones such as:

1 Locate the composter in a place protected from the elements and near the sources of organic matter.
2 Add the waste materials as they become available but still aim to interlayer fine materials with bulky ones and dry with wet.
3 From time to time add a layer of old compost or manure.
4 It is a good idea to aerate the contents by moving them around with the aid of a hook. This is best done when the moon is full.
5 If the mix ever seems dry, water it.
6 Continue filling the container and once it is three-quarters or more full move and mix the contents again.
7 If everything has gone well, the bottom layers will be well fermented and composted in four to six months. The compost should be a dark colour with a loose, homogenous texture and agreeable smell. It is now ready to use on the garden.
8 A composting container which has a door at the bottom can have the mature compost at the bottom removed while new layers of fresh organic material continue to be added to the top.

Topping up a compost bin made of slatted wood.

Compost bins made of wood, plastic and recycled plastic.

Worm composting

If the organic matter available is almost exclusively kitchen waste, a wormery (using red worms) is an interesting option. On the market are some simple and practical models which work using interchangeable trays. A wormery occupies little space and causes no unpleasant smells, making it possible to have one close to the kitchen.

IRRIGATION

Water is the blood of the earth and, of course, of plants. It is the most basic of liquids, precious and versatile. It can be ionized, frozen, evaporated, polarized or charged with electricity, or have substances dissolved in it. Most biological processes depend on it and with air, earth and fire it is one of the four classic elements. Dissolved in water, nutrients present in the soil can be taken up by plant roots and even by leaves, thanks to the air´s humidity. Water also allows and stimulates the proliferation of micro-organisms and mycorrhiza, which assimilate the 'raw' chemical elements and feed them to plants.

Most garden vegetables need a considerable amount of water to develop well. It is important to have an understanding of the water needs of each plant during the different periods of growth. Clearly a lettuce does not have the same requirements as an orange tree or a rose bush. Gardening technique needs to be adapted to allow the best management and most efficient use of water.

Micro-sprinklers make effective use of the available water.

Flood irrigation, the traditional method in many Mediterranean countries, is an inefficient use of water.

How much water and how often?

This is an important subject, somewhat complicated because of the great variety of plants grown in a garden and the specific characteristics and water needs during each growth period of each plant. Even within the same plant family, different varieties can have different needs. For example, salad tomatoes need more watering than varieties grown for preserving, while 'hanging' tomatoes, which are harvested in July/August, require minimal watering if they are to last until January.

In general, juicy vegetables and those with broad leaves tend to need more abundant and regular watering than those with narrow leaves, which can normally do with less. However, it is almost impossible to give guidelines on how much water and how often, as this depends not only on the needs of each specific plant but also on the local climate. Obviously in hot, dry, windy regions watering needs to be more frequent than in cold, damp, rainy ones.

Another factor is the structure and texture of the earth. Clay soil retains water well, to the point that it can tend towards flooding, which in turn can cause root asphyxiation. A stony, sandy soil, on the other hand, drains very easily and needs more regular watering. A good amount of organic matter added to the soil acts like a sponge and helps water retention. It improves both clay and sand soils.

The planting density also influences irrigation needs. Although in principle plants grown close together need more water per square metre than those spaced further apart, you should take into account the fact that the shade cast by the plants slows evaporation (water evaporates rapidly from bare earth under a hot sun), so that in fact they need watering less often. Too much water is harmful, in that it both leaches nutrients from the soil and stimulates the appearance of fungal diseases. It also forces the plant to absorb more water than is really necessary for its correct development: it grows faster but also becomes weaker and more vulnerable to inclement weather, diseases and pests. In addition, overwatering causes the plant to lose flavour and nutritional quality in general.

Observation and experience are the great secrets of correct irrigation. If in doubt, observe and ask local gardeners, and study the water needs of each plant in its different phases of growth.

Irrigation methods

Drip irrigation and micro-sprinklers both provide good results with minimum water use. Drip irrigation is based either on porous pipes or on tubing pierced by emitters that allow the water to drip out at regular intervals. Both drip irrigation and micro-sprinkler systems can be adjusted to supply each plant with the ideal level of humidity at all times and can be regulated throughout the plant's period of growth.

Flood irrigation in furrows or channels gives poor results in terms of water consumed per hectare. It provides a large quantity of water on specific days but leaves the plants thirsty for long periods in between.

Water seeping from porous pipes keeps the soil moist. Here, a watering can provides a top-up for newly planted lettuces.

Drip irrigation systems

There are numerous options when it comes to drip irrigation systems. It is best to opt for systems that have proved themselves to be efficient and are easy to get hold of (including all the parts: connections, stopcocks, filters, etc.). There are shops that specialize in selling irrigation systems to farmers where prices are cheaper than at garden centres or DIY stores.

Tubing

The most commonly found tubing tends to be of flexible black polythene, which is versatile and long lasting. You will need various thicknesses: 25–33mm

Laying pressure-compensating drip irrigation tubing.

Water-saving techniques

In vegetable gardening it is traditional to weed and hoe between plants in the early stages of growth. This serves both to retain soil humidity (disturbed earth acts like a mulch) and to eliminate weeds when they are still small enough to have trouble rerooting. Depending on the climate, the plants and the soil, this can save having to irrigate for a couple of weeks or so.

In dry areas that cannot be irrigated it is customary to use a harrow to break the capillarity of the ground. This is commonly done, with good results, in vineyards and in the cultivation of almond, olive and carob trees. The technique consists of going over the ground with a cultivator or harrow a few days after it has rained, in order to break up the topsoil, which has a tendency towards compaction. Compaction creates minute capillaries through which water retained in the soil rapidly evaporates, aided by solar radiation. By breaking up the soil and disrupting the capillary pores it is possible to retain water at the level of plants' roots for a longer period.

Mulching the ground with organic matter such as straw or harvest remains (or, in specific cases, volcanic rock or stones) prevents excessive water evaporation and results in big water savings. For more on mulching, see page 43.

for the main water outlet, 18–25mm for the main feed or distribution tube to the beds and, lastly, 12, 16 or 18mm tube (see below) with drip holes for the irrigation of the beds or furrows. The price of the tubing depends on the quality (new or recycled polythene) and the thickness of the tube walls. Porous pipes generally give better results when there is sufficient water pressure but the price is relatively high compared to that of drip irrigation tubes.

- If you have low water pressure (less than 1kg) it is best to use 18mm pressure-compensating drip irrigation tubing with 25–35cm between holes.
- For water pressure between 1 and 3kg you can

use 16mm-diameter tubes. Above 3kg you can use either 16mm (easier to find) or 12mm tubes. The ideal distance between holes is 25–35cm. Another option when there is high water pressure is porous pipe.

- It is important to work out the volume of water coming from the holes, as some irrigation tubes are made to drip at a rate of 2 litres of water per hour, while others drip at a rate of 4 litres per hour. This is only a general guide, as how much water actually drips out depends on the water pressure of your water source inlet. The easiest way to work out the volume of water dripping out is to

Lime in water

In hard-water areas, an accumulation of lime in the drip irrigation system can block tubes and drips. Protecting the tubes from the sun by covering them with a straw or green mulch helps keep the tubes damp. This prevents the water near the drips from evaporating too rapidly and leaving patches of crystallized lime. Where the problem is acute, placing magnets at the beginning of the tubes normally helps prevent lime crystallization. To dissolve lime, the tubes can be rolled up and put in a container with vinegar. However, a cheaper and more practical solution is to buy new tubes every five or six years, or whenever they stop working properly. The old ones can be recycled.

Crystallized lime on irrigation tubing.

Porous tubing.

put an empty 1 litre bottle or container under one of the holes and time how long it takes to fill (for example, if it takes 15 minutes to fill the bottle, then the system is dripping at a rate of 4 litres an hour; if it takes half an hour to fill, then the rate is 2 litres per hour). Normally 2 litres per hour will be sufficient, unless you have a very sandy, porous soil, in which case 4 litres per hour is preferable.

- If the garden is sloping or has differences in level, it is best to opt for pressure-compensating drip irrigation tubes (these usually drip at 2 litres per hour). This is because the water spreads itself out better and should irrigate the lowest and highest parts of the beds or furrows equally.

- Porous piping, either rigid or flexible, has the advantage of distributing the water more evenly. The disadvantages are that it is more expensive and does not work well when water pressure is low. It also gets blocked more easily when there are high levels of lime in the water.

Nozzles and emitters

Here again there are numerous options, from individual emitters that need to be connected to the tubes by hand to tubing with factory-installed internal emitters. The advantage of the latter is that it can be easily moved, whereas tubing with external emitters tends to get caught and break.

Where the ground has differences in level of 1.5m or more it is important to use pressure-compensating emitters to avoid some plants receiving more water than others. In irrigation systems where there is not a good filter the emitters get clogged up easily. In this case external emitters are better, as they can be taken apart and cleaned, unlike internal emitters.

To install the emitters, make a hole in the drip tubing using a hole punch. Then press the barbed emitter inlet into the hole where the barb will lock it in place. Because the polythene drip tube is elastic, it will stretch around the barb, sealing itself around the stem of the barb. The hole punched in the tubing should not be bigger than the diameter of the barb stem. When the hole is larger than the barb stem, the hole won't seal and there will be a leak. If the emitter manufacturer makes a special punch, it is advisable to use it, as it will make holes of the right size. If a special hole punch is not available, a battery-operated drill with the right-size drill bit gives good results. Otherwise a nail can be used, but make sure that the diameter of the hole made is not bigger than the stem on the emitter barb. Be careful to punch the hole through one side of the tube only; it is easy to go all the way through one side of the tube and out the other.

It is a good idea to buy some goof plugs. Goof plugs are small plastic barbed plugs used to fill holes that get punched in the wrong place. An emitter installed in the wrong place can simply be pulled out and a goof plug put in the hole. A goof plug has a larger barb

Drip irrigation tubing laid out in a bed.

and stem than most emitters, which is how it fills the old stretched-out holes without leaking. Avoid pulling out goof plugs, as the barb is so large that it often rips the tubing and ruins it. The only solution then is to cut out a section of tubing and splice in a new piece of tube, using two tubing couplings.

Filters

An essential element of a drip irrigation system is the filter (or filters). This is positioned before the timing device or program (if you are using one) and before the distribution tubes or main feed. The filter retains the impurities that would otherwise block the emitters. There are many filters on the market, ranging from simple to complicated and from small to big (better to err on the side of big). The simplest filters normally contain a metal mesh. More expensive but more effective and easier to clean are those made up of disks.

If the water comes from a tank or an irrigation canal, where algae can develop, special sand filters need to be put in to retain the algae. It is important to be conscientious about cleaning the filters once a week or every fifteen days. Take the filters apart and scrub with a brush. Submerge the disk filters in running water, preferably at pressure.

Irrigation programs

There are irrigation programs on the market that vary from the very basic to the very complicated. The most basic type has only one inlet and outlet and works with an electric valve operated by a 9V battery. This type needs only to be connected up and programmed. More complicated programs might have six or more individualized outlets and complex computer programs that can even be connected to meteorological stations or sensors pushed into the ground. These respond from moment to moment to regulate the irrigation automatically. They can even be programmed to irrigate every crop differently and controlled from a computer in the house.

In most cases the most basic type of program will be sufficient. Batteries need to be checked regularly, as if they run out the valve will remain closed and the plants will not be watered.

External emitters.

Filter.

Drip irrigation program.

Tee, ell, tubing, stopcock, coupling.

External emitter.

Using a hole punch to make a hole for an external emitter.

Connecting point between main tube and tube to individual bed.

Other equipment

Apart from hose, drip tube and controllers you will need stopcocks to open and close the irrigation system. A big stopcock is needed for the main hose and other smaller ones that are the thickness of the drip tubes (normally 16mm) for each drip line or bed. You will also need various fittings, including tees, couplings, ells and adapters. These plastic connectors are used to attach the drip tubes to other tubes, control valves or pipes. It is important to make sure the fittings are exactly the right size. Using fittings made for a different tubing size will result in the tube blowing out of the fitting. Remember, both 15mm and 16mm tubes are often labelled as ½-inch size. You really need to know which it is you require.

Drip irrigation installation for a garden arranged in beds

The main tube comes underground from the water tank or outlet to the beds. Each of the drip irrigation tubes in each bed has a tee and stopcock so that they can be turned on and off as needed. A program is installed according to water pressure and irrigation requirements.

1 Water outlet with stopcock
2 Mesh or disk filter
3 Irrigation program
4 25–33mm diameter tube for the main feed. This should be the length of the garden plus the distance to the main stopcock (1).
5 16mm diameter tube without drip holes.
6 Special connections to link the main tube (4) with the 16mm tubes that feed each bed (9).
7 16mm polythene tees for each bed.
8 One or more 16mm stopcocks per bed.
9 16mm drip irrigation tubes with holes every 25–35cm. To calculate the number of metres of tube needed, multiply the length of each bed by the number of tubes needed and multiply the result by the number of beds to be irrigated. For example, 4 tubes x 5m long = 20m; 20m x 6 beds = 120m of tube. It is always best to have a few metres extra, just in case, so in this example buy, say, 125m of tube rather than 120m.
10 Stoppers or end caps to close off the tubes (the tubes can also be crimped over and tied).

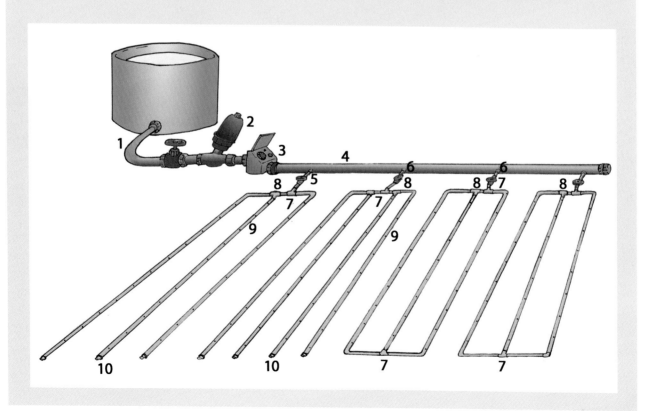

Irrigating a terrace or balcony

If you have an outside tap you can install an automatic irrigation system with a programmer and tubes with one or more emitter in each plant pot or container. Another option (and where there is no outside tap) is to install a 100–200 litre rainwater collection tank and connect that to the irrigation system. In times of drought or scarce rainfall the tank can be filled by hose from a tap in the house.

A terrace garden may well be too small to justify an irrigation system and it might make more sense to use a watering can or hosepipe. However, if you want to be able to go away for a few days or spend less time watering you will need to automate the system. One alternative is irrigation by capillary action. This can be achieved by using ceramic cones inside the plant pots that are connected to tubes submerged in a container filled with water.

A raised container that is irrigated automatically.

Piping to supply water to a raised container.

A wide range of plants growing in a balcony container.

An irrigation system for a built-in planting trough.

Drainage is as important to plants as irrigation.

Gardeners who water by hand get to know their plants well.

Tiered planting is attractive but laborious to water.

PLANT PROPAGATION

You can, of course, buy seeds and plants, but it is more interesting and satisfying to save your own seeds and propagate from plant cuttings.

Seeds

You can use standard commercial seeds to start with, but in time try to move on to using certified organic seeds and to saving your own seeds.

To save very small seeds, wrap a fine mesh or bag around the flower heads while the plants are still in the ground. Do this before they are ripe, to prevent them being lost. Rub fleshy fruit such as tomatoes with a piece of strong cotton cloth and leave to dry. Keep seeds in a cool, dry, ventilated place. For more on seed saving, see page 148.

You can also approach organic gardeners or seed-swapping groups, or exchange seeds with friends, thus helping to save varieties that might otherwise be lost. These might have resistance properties or scents not found in modern varieties. Commercial seed producers limit themselves to varieties suitable for agribusiness, which has very different needs.

You can make your own seed trays from wooden boxes or by recycling small containers such as yoghurt pots and boxes used in packaging. To germinate seeds, it helps to know the process by which their dormancy is broken (the conditions of humidity, cold or heat they require, for instance).

Sowing

Depending on the plant, seeds can be sown under cover, or in unprotected seedbeds, or directly in the ground where the plants are to grow. Sowing seeds in seedbeds or containers is recommended for:

Aubergines (eggplants)	Melons
Cabbages and cauliflowers	Onions
Celery	Peppers
Cucumbers	Squash
Escarole	Swiss chard
Leeks	Tomatoes
Lettuces	Watermelons

Simplifying protected seedbeds

Gardeners often overcomplicate matters, making elaborate hotbeds, and even using electrical heating elements, all for a few tomato or pepper plants which could perfectly well be grown in ordinary plant pots or recycled containers placed on a sunny windowsill. The combination of the sun's heat and that of the home provides more than enough for the plants to germinate and for their initial development. Later they can be pricked out and planted on in new pots or directly in the open, conditions permitting.

Sow seed in trays or recycled containers.

Seedlings in a modular tray, ready for pricking out.

Pricking out seedlings with a forked stick.

Recycled containers for pricking out seedlings.

Firming seedlings gently into growing medium.

For whether to sow in an open seedbed, protected seedbed or hotbed, see table on pages 56–7.

Sowing directly in the ground is the usual procedure for:

Beetroot	Parsnips
Broad (fava) beans	Peas
Carrots	Potatoes
Sweetcorn (corn)	Radishes
Garlic	Spinach
Green (string, flat pole) beans	

Seeds can be scattered freely, or in rows, or in small separate holes. With the seeds of many plants (though not all) you can initially sow very densely, so long as you later prick out the seedlings to give them room to develop. The depth seeds should be sown is normally indicated on the seed packet, but a rule of thumb is to bury them at a depth three times their size. To sow very fine seeds, mix the seeds well with fine, light-coloured sand and spread the mix on the darker coloured, levelled soil. This way the distribution of the seeds shows up clearly.

Sowing medium Garden soil is not suitable as a sowing medium, as it tends to be too coarse and compacts easily. A good sowing medium is one that is not too rich in nutrients and retains humidity well but at the same time is porous enough to allow aeration. Peat is commonly used but should be avoided, as peat reserves are threatened. Coconut fibre is a good substitute for peat, and an ideal mix would be 50 per cent coconut fibre, 40 per cent worm compost (see page 27) and 10 per cent coarse sand. Also suitable is 1 part coarse sand to 2 parts sieved leafmould (rotted-down leaves), or equal parts sieved compost, soil and sand.

Sowing in a seedbed The advantages of sowing in a seedbed are many. Plants can be started off while beds are still occupied with other crops, and the seeds can be sown more densely (for transplanting later), thus saving space. In a protected seed bed (i.e. a seedbed covered with glass, perspex or transparent plastic) humidity and temperature can be more easily controlled, and seeds and seedlings can be protected from being eaten by slugs and snails. Young plants can

Hotbeds and other protected beds

A hotbed is a protected seedbed that has a heat source additional to the sun. The heat is produced by the fermentation of a thick layer of fresh horse, donkey or mule manure. The fermentation is rapid and intense because of the high cellulose content of the straw that is normally mixed in with manure.

The basic idea is to create a box, preferably insulated, with a glass or plastic top, orientated south. A simple method is to dig a hole in the ground $1m^2/11ft^2$ by 30cm/12in deep, orientated south. Fill this with 20cm/8in of fresh horse manure, level it but do not compact, and water well. On top of this lay a 10cm/4in layer of mature compost mixed with leafmould and water again (always water before sowing, not after). Cover with a mini-greenhouse. You can make this from old windows or a cane frame with transparent plastic (preferably the kind used for greenhouses, which deteriorates less rapidly) stapled on to it. A hinge for the top opening door is a good idea. Around the hotbed lay a circle of old roof tiles containing a sprinkling of iron sulphate against snails and slugs, and inside the hotbed lay some bits of cane. Check the canes daily for earwigs, which you should remove. Also check the moisture level in the bed: it must not be allowed to dry out.

Sow seeds densely – e.g. tomatoes 1.5cm/½in apart, courgettes (zucchini) 8cm/3in apart – in rows 10cm/4in apart and transplant to containers or directly outside when big enough. Check for snail lines in the condensation on the plastic and remove any snails you find. When sowing, intersperse tomatoes, which insects do not like, with peppers, which are more vulnerable to attack. If for any reason, such as weather, transplanting is delayed, you can always water the hotbed with water that has had manure soaked in it.

Another cheap way to make the structure, whether for a protected seedbed or a hotbed, is by using straw bales as walls. Fill the space inside the straw bale walls with horse manure as above or just potting compost, or simply place the seed trays inside. Cover with a sheet of plastic or glass. Double sheet methacrylate plastic works well, as it is light and unlike glass does not need to be in a frame; however, it is more expensive. The straw eventually breaks down and can be recycled as mulch.

To save work the following year, when you have removed all plants from the hotbed leave the manure to finish decomposing in the bed. The following year the top layer can be sieved and used as potting compost, and the lower layer sieved and spread over a fresh layer of horse manure. For this to work, you must pull out all plants and keep the hotbed free of weeds, as otherwise these will devour the nutrients and leave the compost full of weed seeds.

During periods of hard frost you can protect the seedbed or hotbed by covering it with old blankets, sacks or cardboard weighed down with stones. Remember to remove them as soon as the sun comes up.

Protected seed trays.

A hotbed.

Keep the root ball intact when transplanting.

Transplant young plants into prepared ground.

then be pricked out into individual containers or transplanted into the ground where they are to grow. Only plants that survive transplanting well are suitable for sowing in seedbeds.

Sowing in pots or modular seed trays The advantage of this method is that roots are less likely to be damaged in the process of transplanting. The disadvantage is that seed trays rapidly dry out and need to be constantly watered.

Cuttings

Cuttings should be taken from strong-growing shoots on cool, damp days. Take cuttings from summer-flowering plants in spring and vice versa. The average length of cuttings should be some 15cm/6in.

It is easy and cheap to make a covered container for seeds and cuttings. Simply cover a wooden or polystyrene box with a plastic bag supported on semicircles of wire to make a mini-polytunnel.

Make a low-nutrient sowing medium that is aerated and drains well by using a base of compost, soil and sand in equal parts.

To encourage the development of roots, make a shallow cut in the base of the cutting and insert a grain of corn into the cut. When the corn germinates, it will produce enzymes that will be helpful to the roots. Another method is to soak the cuttings in water in which willow branches and compost have been macerated. Before transplanting it is advisable to wet the new plants with a solution of compost water and whole milk diluted 1 to 10, which acts as a fungicide.

Plant the cuttings in a covered container and maintain the soil at a uniform humidity. Cuttings produce roots in three to six weeks depending on temperature and humidity.

Plant out in autumn or spring; water first so that the soil adheres well to the roots.

Layering

Layering is the process of burying part of a branch in damp soil so that it produces roots; later you cut the connection to the mother plant. Layering is done by cutting or twisting the end or part of the branch to be layered in order to stop the flow of hormones and other organic composites that normally accumulate at the branch´s end. Root development is stimulated by the absence of light and the increased flow of sap. The best time for layering is between autumn and spring.

Plant division

Perennial plants can be propagated by dividing them into pieces, each with a root system and one or more shoots or buds. Plant division is best done in late autumn or early spring when the plant is dormant. It should not be done in extremely cold, wet or dry weather when it is more difficult for the divided plants to re-establish successfully. Lift the plant to be divided, taking care to insert the fork far enough away so as not to damage the roots. You can separate plants by chopping them into pieces with a spade if woody, or easing pieces apart by hand. The divided sections can then be replanted.

PLANT PROTECTION

Intense cold, strong winds, certain pests, excessive humidity – these factors can cause serious damage in the garden. To minimize their impact, it is sometimes necessary, especially in less propitious regions, to introduce some form of protection.

Cold

Cold slows down plant growth but is also a great controller of pests and disease. The problem is that intense cold and frosts also damage garden plants. There are many unlucky regions where a climate of short summers and long winters curtails enormously the supply of fresh vegetables for many months of the year.

Greenhouses Greenhouses, whether made of plastic or glass, are a good alternative where a cold climate limits the growing season. The growing conditions in a greenhouse are a little forced and plants tend to accumulate more nitrogen than those grown outside. However, between eating your own organic lettuces in December and buying lettuces from shops, the choice is clear.

Tunnels Plastic tunnels are easy to make and can provide vital protection to plants as winter passes to spring. They make it possible to bring forward the planting out of plants sensitive to cold and wind such as tomatoes, aubergines (eggplants), peppers, courgettes (zucchini) and melons. In cold regions they provide a means of prolonging the harvest of lettuces and escarole (broad-leaved endive).

Cones or recycled water containers Transparent 5-litre water containers are a simple and effective means of protecting recently sown or transplanted plants. Simply cut off the base and place over the plant.

Windbreaks

Air is vital for plants and good ventilation is important for the garden's health. However, too much air, in the form of strong winds or gusts of cold Siberian air, can be disastrous. It is useful to know from which direction strong or cold winds might come so that you can grow hedges or put up some kind of windbreak in the most critical season.

A polytunnel consisting of a frame and plastic sheeting.

Recycled water containers protect transplanted plants.

Barriers against pests

In some gardens it is necessary to make traps or some kind of barrier to protect the plants from snails and slugs. In others a fence is essential against rabbits and hares.

Vines and fruit trees might need to be covered in nets to stop birds getting at the fruit.

An interesting example of a protective barrier on the island of La Palma in the Canaries consists of a thin metal sheet with the top inclined outwards. This stops lizards getting in and devouring all the fresh vegetables for the water contained in them.

For more on pest control, see pages 50 and 149.

MULCHING

Mulching is an excellent strategy. A permanent cover of straw or other organic material protects the ground from both intense solar radiation and rapid water evaporation. It is especially effective in hot, dry climates with plenty of sun.

Advantages of mulching

- By protecting the soil from intense solar radiation, mulching prevents ultraviolet light from destroying or damaging bacterial and microbial flora in the ground under cultivation.
- It stops the ground from drying out, thus helping to keep the soil moist and considerably reducing the need for irrigation.
- The shade provided by the mulch not only maintains the soil's moisture but also prevents weed growth.
- Mulching helps aeration because mulch is porous and it protects the soil from compaction.
- A mulch shades the soil and surface compost, creating a microclimate that facilitates microbial flora activity, especially that of nitrogen-fixing bacteria. These bacteria, under a layer of mulch, can absorb from the air up to 80kg/176lb of nitrogen per hectare/2½ acres per year and fix it in the soil.

Limitations of mulching

Despite the undeniable advantages of mulching there are times when it is not advisable. Mulching is not applicable for all plants or for all climates. Whereas plants may be mulched, seeds need the soil to be clear and exposed to light. Where mulching is perhaps most controversial is in cold, damp regions. These, while having hot summers, normally have cool springs. Mulch-covered soil fails to heat up enough to stimulate growth and maximize fruit production. The plants most affected are from the solanaceae family (such as tomatoes, peppers and aubergines/eggplants) and cucurbits (melons and watermelons). In cold regions with short summers best results are obtained by leaving the soil exposed to the heat of the sun.

A good way of protecting the soil while still allowing it to warm up is to cover it (or surface compost) with mature leafmould, well-rotted manure or the remains of seedbeds (mixtures of compost, leafmould, coconut fibre). These materials, being dark, absorb maximum solar radiation while at the same time providing shade and protecting the soil and surface compost from harmful ultraviolet radiation.

Another effective though less ecological option is the use of black shade netting. This is particularly useful in gardens lashed by strong winds or where old leafmould or other organic alternatives are unavailable.

Mulching is particularly beneficial in sunny, dry conditions.

Spreading an even layer of straw as a mulch.

COMPANION PLANTING

An organic garden is, as we have seen, an ecosystem where continual interaction is taking place. It follows that a plant cannot be considered in isolation. The synergy between plants and how they help or hinder each other's development is something to take into consideration. It is reasonable to speculate – and the success of crop rotation points to the same conclusion – that a plant transforms its surroundings through its biological activity and what it exudes. It creates biochemical conditions or stimulates bacterial populations that favour its own development. This biochemical activity is in turn either inhibiting or stimulating to other plants and also has an attracting or repellent effect on certain pests. Traditionally, for example, it is recommended that you plant basil next to peppers and tomatoes to deter aphid attack. Another traditional practice is planting leeks or onions on the borders of beds or rows of carrots to deter carrot fly.

However, this is a little investigated field, and it is well worth observing relations between plants and experimenting with them to see what conclusions can be drawn and how you can apply them. For a table showing plant associations, compiled by the Spanish gardener Carlos García Dolz, see pages 46–7.

Apart from whether plants' secretions are compatible or mutually beneficial, it is common sense not to combine plants with different growing rhythms, soil type preferences or water needs, or plants with competing root systems or above-ground growth.

There are also occasions when one plant helps another simply by its physical form, the way it grows or its resistance. Sweetcorn (corn), courgettes (zucchini), green (string and flatpole) beans and peas are examples of symbiotic growing combinations. The peas and beans provide nitrogen; the courgettes give ground cover; and the sweetcorn acts as a support.

Sweetcorn and beans: a mutually supportive growing combination.

Both lettuces and onions benefit from close association.

CROP ROTATION

One of the keys to a healthy garden is to rotate crops. Growing the same plants in succession in the same place can cause imbalances and use up certain nutrients. This has a negative effect on plant development and can lead to disease and the flourishing of certain pests.

A basic guideline to follow in crop rotation is to follow nutrient-demanding plants with less demanding ones. Follow these with plants with low nutrient needs. Finish the cycle with a soil-improving or fertilizing crop such as legumes or a green manure (see page 46).

Nutrient-demanding plants These are plants which develop well when provided with large quantities of nutrients, such as potatoes, squash, courgettes (zucchini), tomatoes, peppers, aubergines (eggplants), melons, cucumbers, watermelons, cabbages, cauliflowers, sweetcorn (corn), spinach and Swiss chard.

Less demanding plants Some plants, such as lettuces, escarole (broad-leaved endive) and leeks, need good nutrition but grow well after a demanding crop with barely any extra compost. Carrots, beetroot, radishes and parsnips are also in this category but grow best in well-broken-down compost, leafmould or worm compost.

Planting in blocks simplifies rotation.

Rotation by botanical group

Another rotation plan that is easy to follow is to divide up beds according to botanical groups: solanaceae; compositae, chenopodiaciae and cucurbits together; umbelliferae and liliaciae together; legumes and crucifers together. Potatoes, though solanaceae, are usually in a separate bed on their own. Rotate on the principle of less demanding crops following more demanding ones. After soil-improving plants such as legumes, plant a more demanding crop. You need also to plan for some permanent beds of perennials such as artichokes and strawberries.

Bed 1
Solanaceae
Tomatoes
Peppers
Aubergines
(eggplants)

Bed 2
Compositae
Lettuces
Escarole
Chenopodiaciae
Swiss chard
Beetroot
Spinach
Cucurbits
Cucumber
Courgettes (zucchini)

Bed 3
Umbelliferae
Carrots
Celery
Liliaciae
Onions
Leeks

Bed 4
Legumes
Green beans
Peas
Broad beans (fava)
Crucifers
Cabbages
Radishes

Bed 5
Perennials
Artichokes
Strawberries
Asparagus

As marigolds repel various pests, they are useful companion plants.

Peas fix nitrogen in the soil.

Least demanding plants Most of the plants in this category are root plants (such as garlic, onions, radishes) and legumes (peas, green beans/string and flatpole beans, broad/fava beans, soya beans, lentils, lupins). The latter have the ability to absorb and synthesize atmospheric nitrogen and so do not need additional compost.

Soil-improving plants These are plants that, besides being undemanding in nutrients, enrich the soil in which they grow. Apart from the legumes already mentioned, there are what are known as green manures, such as clover, field beans, vetch, sainfoin and alfalfa. These can be grown on their own or mixed in with a graminaceous crop (plants from the grass family).

PLANT ASSOCIATIONS AND ROTATIONS

R = avoid replanting in the same spot within the specified number of years.

	Associations		Rotations (R)	
	FAVOURABLE	UNFAVOURABLE	PREVIOUS	AVOID
ARTICHOKE	lettuce			
ASPARAGUS	cucumber, parsley, leek, pea, tomato	garlic, beetroot, onions		
AUBERGINE (EGGPLANT) R 3 years	green bean	potato	cabbage, carrot, celery, garlic, leek, legumes, lettuce, onion, radish, sweetcorn, turnip	aubergine, cucumber, melon, pepper, potato, squash, tomato
BEAN, BROAD R 4–5 years	potato, sweetcorn, spinach	cabbage	aubergine, carrot, celery, cucumber, garlic, leek, melon, onion, pepper, potato, squash, tomato	legumes
BEAN, GREEN R 2–3 years	aubergine, carrot, celery, cabbage, spinach, strawberry, lettuce, corn, turnip, potato, radish, squash, cucumber, savoury	garlic, beetroot, fennel, onion, Swiss chard, tomato	tomato, pepper, aubergine, potato, celery, carrot, garlic, onion, leek, cucumber, squash, melon	legumes
BEETROOT	cabbage, celery, lettuce, onion	asparagus, carrots, green beans, leeks, tomatoes		
CABBAGE R 5 years	beetroot, celery, lettuce, lamb's lettuce, pea, potato, tomato, spinach, cucumber	garlic, chicory, fennel, leek, radish, onion	garlic, onion, potato, tomato, aubergine, melon, cucumber, squash, watermelon, spinach	cabbage, turnip, radish, carrot, green bean
CARROT	spring onion, green bean, lettuce, onion, leek, pea, radish, tomato, parsley, chervil, garlic	beetroot	legumes	
CELERY	beetroot, cabbage, cucurbits, green bean, leek, Swiss chard, pea, tomato	lettuce, sweetcorn, parsley		
CUCUMBER R 2 years	asparagus, basil, celery, cabbage, spring onion, green bean, lettuce, sweetcorn, pea	potato, radish, tomato	garlic, onion, leek, sweetcorn, celery, carrot, cabbage, radish, lettuce, broad bean, pea, potato, pepper, aubergine	cucumber, squash, courgette, melon, watermelon
FENNEL	celery, leek	cabbage, green bean, tomato		
GARLIC	strawberry, potato, lettuce, tomato	cabbage, green bean, pea	anything except garlic, onion, leek	garlic, onion, leek
KOHLRABI	beetroot, celery, lettuce, leek	chicory, fennel, strawberry, radish		
LAMB'S LETTUCE	cabbage, strawberry, leek			
LEEK	asparagus, carrot, celery, fennel, strawberry, lettuce, onion, tomato	beetroot, cabbage, parsley, Swiss chard, pea		

	Associations		Rotations (R)	
	Favourable	Unfavourable	Previous	Avoid
LETTUCE	beetroot, carrot, chervil, cabbage, cucumber, broad bean, strawberry, turnip, onion, leek, pea, radish, garlic, artichoke, squash, spinach	parsley, sunflower	tomato, aubergine, pepper, celery, carrot, melon, cucumber, squash	lettuce, escarole, cabbage, radish, turnip
MELON AND WATERMELON R 2 years			garlic, onion, leek, corn, celery, carrot, cabbage, radish, lettuce, broad bean, pea, potato, tomato, pepper, aubergine	cucumber, squash, courgette, melon, water melon, tomato
ONION	beetroot, carrot, cucumber, strawberry, lettuce, parsley, leek, tomato, cabbage, chamomile	cabbage, green bean, pea, potato, radish	everything	garlic, onion, leek
PARSNIP	carrot, onion	fennel		
PEA R 4–5 years	asparagus, carrot, celery, cabbage, cucumber, lettuce, sweetcorn, turnip, potato, radish	garlic, onion, leek, parsley	tomato, pepper, aubergine, potato, celery, carrot, garlic, onion, leek, cucumber, squash, melon	legumes
PEPPER R 3 years	basil		garlic, celery, cabbage, onion, legumes, sweetcorn, lettuce, turnip, leek, radish, carrot	squash, melon, cucumber, pepper, tomato, potato, aubergine
POTATO R 3–4 years	garlic, nasturtium, celery, cabbage, legumes, calendula, carrot, radish	aubergine, cucumber, onion, squash, sunflower	garlic, celery, cabbage, onion, legumes, lettuce, turnip, sweetcorn, leek, radish, carrot	squash, melon, cucumber, pepper, tomato, potato, aubergine
RADISH	carrot, chervil, spinach, lettuce, pea, tomato, garlic, cucumber, green bean	cabbage, squash, turnip	garlic, onion, potato, tomato, aubergine, melon, cucumber, squash, watermelon, spinach	cabbage, turnip, radish, carrot, green bean
SPINACH	cabbage, strawberry, green bean, turnip, radish, lettuce	beetroot, Swiss chard		
STRAWBERRY	garlic, chives, spinach, green bean, lettuce, lamb's lettuce, turnip, onion, leek, calendula, thyme	cabbage		
SWEETCORN	cucurbits, legumes, tomato	sunflower, beetroot, garlic, potato		
SWISS CHARD	celery, lettuce, strawberry, green bean, onion	asparagus, leek, tomato		
TOMATO R 3–4 years	garlic, asparagus, basil, nasturtium, carrot, celery, cabbage, carnation, onion, parsley, leek, radish, calendula, sweetcorn	beetroot, kohlrabi, fennel, Swiss chard, pea, green bean, cucumber, potato	garlic, celery, cabbage, legumes, corn, lettuce, turnip, leek, radish, carrot	squash, melon, cucumber, pepper, tomato, potato, aubergine
TURNIP	pea, spinach, green bean, lettuce, cucumber	radish, barley	chicory, fennel, leek, radish	potato, tomato, aubergine, melon, cucumber, squash, watermelon, spinach

COSMIC INFLUENCES AND THE LUNAR CALENDAR

The planet earth exists in a sea of radiations and cosmic energies, of which the strongest source is the sun. As children we are taught that it is the earth that revolves around the sun. However, for the plants in the garden it is the sun, the moon and the stars that revolve around them, constantly changing position and varying the radiations and influences that the plants receive.

The influence the cosmos has on the vital processes of living beings is undeniable, if only for the fact that solar radiation determines the seasonal rhythm of life. It is easy to accept that sunlight and heat, both easily perceptible, have an effect on plant growth (and on people´s moods). Less easy to admit are the possible effects of the moon, despite the fact that since the dawn of humanity people have lived as much in time with the moon as with the sun. Still harder is it to accept that a remote constellation of stars can have a perceptible effect on biological processes and favour or not our plants´ development.

Our attitude to the question of cosmic or lunar influences can be one of complete denial – ignoring what can be observed – or of blind faith with no questions asked. Perhaps the best course is to be open-minded and willing to experiment.

For centuries gardeners have followed the lunar calendar.

Following the lunar calendar

The simplest form of moon planting is that which follows the waxing and waning of the moon, or synodic cycle. The element most clearly affected is water, with a distinct increase in the earth´s moisture content in the forty-eight hours leading up to a full moon.

Some general guidelines for planting by the visible waxing or waning of the moon are given below.

More detailed is the biodynamic cycle developed by Rudolf Steiner in 1924, which works with six moon rhythms, including ascending and descending moon and the moon´s position in front of the zodiac constellations. You can buy detailed calendars for biodynamic planting.

The best moon for each activity

Starting or turning compost	full moon and last quarter
Fertilizing	full or waning moon
Starting plant-based preparations (e.g. nettle tea)	new moon and first quarter
Weeding and digging	last quarter
Pruning	waning moon
Saving seeds	full moon
Transplanting	waxing moon
Grafting	waxing moon
Rooting of cuttings	waning moon
Root development	last quarter

AVOIDING PROBLEMS

Prejudice

There is a prejudice that persists – despite the fact that it does not correspond to reality – that organic agriculture is not viable. It is said that without chemical pesticides the innumerable pests that feed on plants make any attempt to grow vegetables futile; and that without synthetic fertilizers plants become anaemic and give mediocre harvests. From these false premises it is deduced that if farmers were to go organic, insufficient food would be produced and world hunger would increase.

To be a successful organic grower it is important to forget the idea that the soil is some inert matter which functions like a machine on the basis of units of NPK (nitrogen, phosphorous and potassium). The soil is alive and its life is dependent on certain laws. If natural processes are not respected, this life falls into disequilibrium and sickens, producing in turn sick plants. In conventional agriculture the soil suffers severe disequilibrium and produces sick plants. As a consequence, diseases are systematic and devastating, poisoning both plants and soil.

Healthy resistant plants

In order to have healthy plants, the first necessity is a living soil. By encouraging the highly complex framework of biodiversity you enable the soil to transform itself, arriving at a state of inertia that favours and encourages the health of plants growing in it. A healthy plant is less vulnerable to insect attack, disease and pests.

In organic agriculture it can be seen how predators do not attack plants in a logical progression depending on proximity. Instead they 'choose' certain plants. The reason is that plants, like human beings, emit signals into their immediate environment. Other beings in this ecosystem pick up these signals and filter them in search of those that are favourable to them, and provide opportunities for satisfying their needs. Just as a lion reads the movements in a herd of herbivores and detects the sick or weak one as being the most accessible, so a garden pest is alert to

Nests for garden friends.

Garden friends

Birds are great insect devourers, especially during breeding time. Putting up bird feeders and ready-made nests can help increase their presence. To scare them away from trees you want to protect, you can make a silhouette of a cat, or bend a piece of tube to look like a snake, and put it beneath the tree. It has been observed that birds do not like sea creatures, so some farmers hang up dry crabs or herrings to scare them away from fruit trees.

Spiders, centipedes, ladybirds, hoverflies, wasps and frogs also help reduce the population of insect pests, and their presence in the garden should be valued and promoted. Above all, do nothing that might harm them.

The larvae and adults of many ladybird species feed on aphids.

The jug-shaped mud nest of a potter wasp.

Many flowers attract hoverflies, which feed on aphids.

all the signals given off by plants – sounds, colours, reflexes, chemical molecules, frequencies and smells – and, to survive, deciphers this code in order to detect the most suitable victim.

Plagues of pests

When a pest that feeds on plants becomes a plague, its natural predators multiply at the expense of the pest until a new balance is reached. Thus given enough time a plague, which is a sign of an alteration in the subtle equilibrium of an ecosystem, puts in motion a compensating mechanism that neutralizes it.

It follows that if a plague is a symptom of an alteration in the natural equilibrium, the application of pesticides is only going to aggravate this disequilibrium. In conventional agriculture wide-spectrum pesticides are used, which kill many more species than those being targeted. These pesticides also invariably cause more damage to the pest's predators than to the pest itself. In a balanced natural environment all the pests and all their predators coexist. Balance is maintained through their interaction, and the diversity of microbial organisms makes biological control possible. When confronted by a plague, try to eliminate the conditions that favour it and do everything possible to increase the presence of the pest's predators.

Remedies for plague or disease

First you need to look at the problem in an integrated way. What might have caused the plague or disease? Might it be too much or too little water? Or sun? Strong, dry or cold winds? An imbalance in the soil? Problems of adaptation? Poor seeds? Errors in cultivation? What lessons can you learn? Sometimes it is a series of unfavourable weather conditions that has weakened a plant or favoured a pest. In this case you can only wait for environmental factors to balance it out.

In the meantime you may be forced to act. In such a situation choose the action with least impact first, moving on if necessary to other options, in the order given here:

Fruit fly trap.

- Biological control: introducing an antagonistic or predatory species or vegetable whose symbiosis with the cultivated plant protects it from the pest or disease.
- Physical intervention (such as picking off the insects). Get rid of affected parts. Adopt physical measures to stop it spreading (barriers, greased tape on tree trunks, sticky yellow strips, food or pheromone containing traps, etc.).
- Plant-based repellents (such as garlic or worm-wood).
- Natural insecticides that biodegrade rapidly, sprayed or dusted only on infected plants without affecting the rest of the ecosystem (such as pyrethrum, neem).

In all cases it is a good idea to treat plants regularly with a vitalizing nettle and horsetail tea.

For more information on the control of pests and diseases, see page 149.

Competing plants

As far as so-called 'weeds' go, the use of an organic mulch greatly reduces their presence. It also protects the soil and its bacteria from harmful solar radiation and helps to reduce evaporation, thus saving on watering: see page 43.

The instant garden

Fear of the work involved in making a garden and of becoming enslaved by the ongoing maintenance it will require is often the reason for never starting. However, there is a way – pioneered by permaculturists and experimental gardeners – of making an almost instant garden that is easy to construct and productive, and involves barely any effort.

The method is to spread some 2–4cm/¾–1½in of compost or other decomposed organic matter (the more decomposed below, the fresher above) on ground from which you have cleared the surface weeds. Above the compost you lay drip irrigation pipes, preferably connected to a watering program, and above that some 4–6cm/1½–2½in of straw or pine needles. A layer of cardboard, preferably plain, below the straw is an additional aid in suppressing stronger weeds in the first year. And that's all! The ground is ready for you to transplant tomatoes, peppers, Swiss chard, courgettes, lettuces or whatever other plant into it (if using cardboard, make a small incision in the cardboard where the plant is to go). You can use the same method around fruit trees, as the lack of digging means that no harm is done to the roots.

This system reduces all work, prevents evaporation and hinders competitive weeds from coming up. One disadvantage is that root crops such as carrots might suffer from the presence of large stones in the soil. Once a year, in spring or autumn, lift up the mulch and add a layer of compost or decaying organic matter. Return the mulch, maybe adding to it if it has diminished over time.

Take heart, all you lazy people out there: plentiful harvests await you!

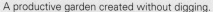

A productive garden created without digging.

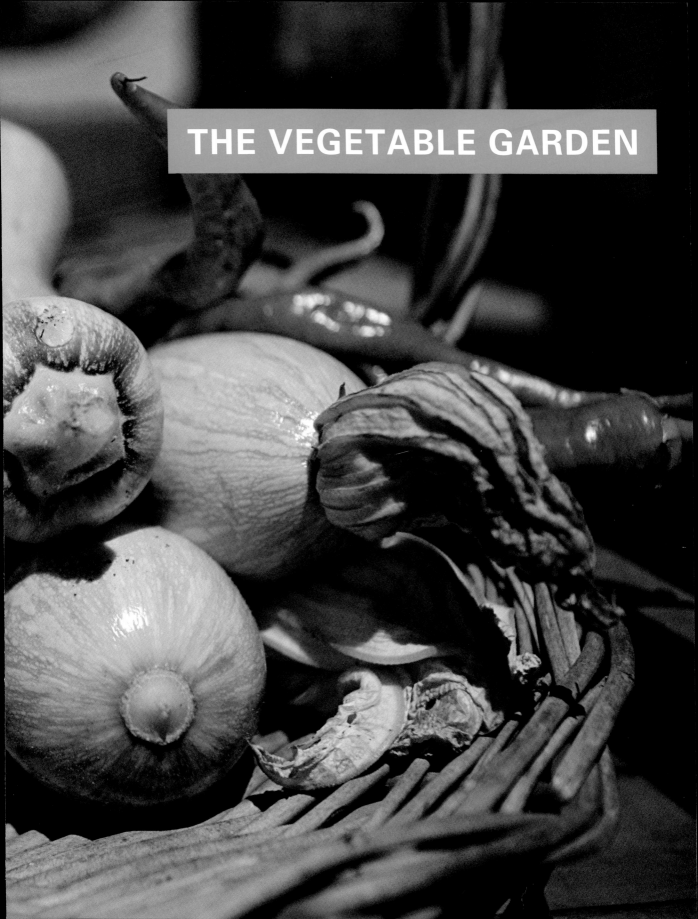

THE VEGETABLE GARDEN

CALENDAR OF SOWING AND HARVESTING

Adapting the dates for your region
The dates given here for sowing, transplanting and harvesting take as their reference temperate regions of the Mediterranean, where the climate is stable for most of the year, with warm winters and summers that rarely reach very high temperatures. The dates are based on Castellon in Valencia, Spain (latitude 39.98).

Given the variations in climate in different geographical regions, every gardener should adjust the dates according to their own regional climate. For further explanation of climate zones, see page 19.

Hot zones In hot zones the best time for sowing and transplanting can be two weeks to a month before the dates indicated in the table.

Cold regions Dates for sowing and transplanting are likely to be two weeks to a month, or even six weeks, behind those given in the table. This will depend on geographic location and the severity of the winters (for more on last and first frosts, see page 19). The harvesting period will also be shorter.

Note: Some vegetables, such as artichokes, broad beans and escarole that are generally grown in autumn/winter in hot regions, are usually summer crops in cold regions.

Season groupings across the months: Winter (January–February), Spring (March–May), Summer (June–August), Autumn (September–December). Each month is divided into two halves, labelled 1 and 2.

VEGETABLES	Jan 1	Jan 2	Feb 1	Feb 2	Mar 1	Mar 2	Apr 1	Apr 2	May 1	May 2	Jun 1	Jun 2	Jul 1	Jul 2	Aug 1	Aug 2	Sep 1	Sep 2	Oct 1	Oct 2	Nov 1	Nov 2	Dec 1	Dec 2
ARTICHOKE	H	H	H	H	H	H							T	T	T	T	T	T			H	H	H	H
ASPARAGUS			S	S	S H	S H	H	H	H															
AUBERGINE (eggplant)					C	C	CT	ST	ST	ST	T	T		H	H	H	H	H	H	H	H	H	H	H
BEAN, BROAD (fava)	H	H	H		S H	S H	S H	H	H	H	H						S	S	S	S			H	H
BEAN, CLIMBING					S	S	S	S	S	S	S	S	S H	S H	H	H	H	H	H	H	H			
BEAN, DWARF					C	C	S	S	S	S	S	S	S	S	S H	S H	H	H	H	H	H	H	H	
BEETROOT			S H	S H	ST H	ST H	ST H	ST H	ST H	ST H	ST H	ST H	T H	H	H	H	S H	S H	S H	ST H	ST H	T H	H	H
BROCCOLI	H	H	H	H	H	H			S	S	ST	ST	ST	ST	ST	ST	T	T	T		H	H	H	H
BRUSSELS SPROUT	H	H	H						S	S	S	S	ST	ST	ST	ST	ST	T	T H	T H	H	H	H	H
CABBAGE (dense-headed)	C H	C H	CT H	CT H	ST H	ST H	ST H	ST H	ST H	ST H	ST H	ST H	ST H	T H	T H	H	S H	S H	ST H	ST H	ST H	ST H	ST H	ST H
CABBAGE (loose-headed)	H	H	H	H	H	H	S	S	S	ST	ST	T	T	T			S H	S H	ST H	ST H	T H	H	H	H
CARROT			S H	S H	S H	S H	S H	S H	S H	S H	S H	S H	H	H	H	H	S H	S H	S H	S H	H	H	H	H
CAULIFLOWER	H	H	H	H	H	H	H	H	H		S	ST	ST	ST	ST	ST	ST	ST H	ST H	ST H	T H	T H	T H	T H
CELERY	H	H	H	H	C H	S H	S	S	S	ST	ST	ST	ST	ST	T	T	T	S H	S H	ST H	ST H	T H	H	H
COURGETTE (zucchini)					C	CT	CT	ST	ST	ST	ST	ST	ST	T H	T H	H	H	H	H	H	H	H	H	H
CUCUMBER					C	C	CT	CT	ST	ST	ST	ST	ST	T	T H	H	H	H	H	H	H	H	H	
ENDIVE	H	H	H	H	H	H	C	C	S	S	S												H	H
ESCAROLE (broad-leaved endive)	ST H	ST H	T H	T H	H	H	H	H	H	H	H	H			S	S	ST H	ST H	ST H	ST H	ST H	ST H	ST H	ST H
FENNEL					C	C	CT	CT	ST	ST	T H	T H	T H	T H			S	S	ST H	ST H	T H	T H		
GARLIC	S	S	S	S							H	H	H	H	H	H	H	H	S	S	S	S		

Planting & harvesting calendar

	JAN	FEB	MAR	APR	MAY	JUN	JUL	AUG	SEP	OCT	NOV	DEC
	Winter			Spring			Summer			Autumn		
KOHLRABI	H	H	C	S	ST	ST		H	H	H	H	H
LAMB'S LETTUCE	H	H						S	S	S/H	H	H
LEEK	H	C/H	CT/H	ST/H	ST/H	T/H	T/H	H	S/H	ST/H	ST/H	T/H
LETTUCE	C/H	CT/H	ST/H	ST/H	ST/H	ST/H	ST/H	ST/H	ST/H	ST/H	ST/H	S/H
MELON			C	ST	ST	ST/T	T/H	H	H			
ONION		C	C	C/CT/H	CT/T/H	T	T	S	S/H	H	T	T
PARSLEY	H	C/H	C/ST/H	ST/H	ST/H	ST/H	ST/H	ST/H	ST/H	ST/H	T/H	T/H
PARSNIP	C	C	C	C/S	S	S/H	H	H	H	H		
PEA			S/H	S/H	S/H	H	H		S	S	S/H	S/H
PEPPER		C	C	CT	ST	ST/H	T/H	H	H	H		
POTATO	S	S	S	S	S/H	H	H		S	S	H	H
RADISH	S/H	S/H	S/H	S/H	S/H	S/H	S/H	S/H	S/H	S/H	S/H	S/H
SPINACH	C/H	C/H	C/S/H	S/H	S/H	H	H		S	S/H	S/H	S/H
SQUASH			C	C/S	ST	ST/T	H	H	H			
STRAWBERRY	CT	CT	CT	CT/H	H	H	H	H		T	T	
SUNFLOWER				S	S	S	S	H	H	H		
SWEETCORN				S	S	S	S/H	H	H	H		
SWISS CHARD	H	C/H	C/H	C/ST/H	ST/H	ST/H	ST/H	ST/H	S/H	ST/H	ST/H	T/H
TOMATO	C	C	C	C/CT	CT/ST	ST/ST	T/H	H	H	H	H	H
TURNIP	H	H	H	S/H	S/H	S/H	H	H	S	S	H	H
WATERMELON			C	CT	ST	ST/T/H	T/H	H	H			

Key

S Sow outside

C Sow under cover

T Transplant

ST Sow and/or transplant outside

CT Sow and/or transplant under cover

H Harvest

Artichoke

In hot and temperate climates artichokes are the queens of the garden in winter and spring. In cold climates they are enjoyed in spring and the beginning of summer. The flower bud is the part of the plant eaten, and its properties and exquisite taste make it worthy of being grown in every garden.

Site and soil Artichokes are greedy plants and need plenty of dug-in manure, as well as regular additions of well-broken-down compost. They like open, loose soils, rich in humus and very fertile. They are a bit particular as regards climatic conditions, as they tolerate neither frosts nor excessive heat. For this reason they are grown from the end of summer to the beginning of spring in hot regions and from March to July or August in cold regions.

The artichoke is a plant that lasts two or three years in the same place. It needs regular top dressing with manure or compost during its reproductive phase and when it thins out at the end of summer before sprouting again in autumn.

It needs frequent watering but does not tolerate excessive humidity, which rots the roots. It suffers badly from dehydration when watering is neglected.

Cultivation The usual way to propagate artichoke plants is by taking offsets (shoots with attached roots

taken from the outer section of the established plant). The central stem will not produce more shoots, so every year you should take some offsets from the established plant, leaving two or three to renew the plant.

The most practical and effective way to cultivate artichokes is to plant them in rows or beds 70cm/27in apart with 70cm/27in between rows, covering the soil with 3–5cm/1¼–2in of compost. If you install a system of drip irrigation and put a good layer of mulch on top, you need hardly think about them again until harvest time.

Care and maintenance Artichokes produce one large central bud and then several lateral buds (three to five, depending on variety and time of planting), which progressively diminish in size. After cutting the third artichoke it is a good idea to remove the mulch and apply a new layer of compost, covering again with mulch. This replenishes the nutrients in the soil and the plant, thus maintaining constant production of good-sized artichokes.

Aphid attack – which may occur when there is a change in the weather or as a result of the application of too much manure or fresh compost – can be controlled by making favourable conditions for earwigs (see page 149) or resorting to using potassium soap or other organic control methods.

In full summer stop watering the plants, so that they dry out. From July, August or September cut down the central stem and begin again the process of thinning out and replanting.

When budding begins, the spaces left empty between plants can be planted with lettuces. In September in the spaces left empty because the plants have not produced shoots you can sow broad (fava) beans. These grow very well when planted alongside artichokes.

Aubergine (eggplant)

Aubergines are the only plants of the solanaceae family that have come to us from Asia rather than America. As with other solanaceae, aubergines love light, sun and above all heat, which is essential to their growth and production. Sowing and care and maintenance are similar to those described for tomatoes (page 79). Sowing is normally delayed until February or March (depending on climate and region), as aubergines require more hours of light and heat than tomatoes or peppers.

Site and soil Deep, fertile soil is needed. Ideally transplant into beds with a layer of compost covered by a deep mulch. In cool springs delay laying the mulch until May or June, so that the ground and the roots of the plant have a chance to warm up, thus speeding the plant´s development.

Space plants 60–70cm/24–27in apart with 70–90cm/27–36in between rows.

Some gardeners cut back the central stem when the plant is 50cm/20in high. This accelerates the development of lateral branches, inducing earlier flowering and increased production.

Aubergines need abundant regular watering (especially at the height of summer). If beds have been prepared with plenty of compost, there is no need to add more during the fruiting period, although in regions with long growing seasons it helps to water plants with diluted juice from a wormery.

In hot regions when winter cold arrives plants are given a general pruning and covered with straw. This way the plants sprout again in winter and produce more fruit.

Bean, broad (fava)

Broad beans are valuable for their protein content. They tolerate moderate frost (–3˚C/27˚F) but not excessive heat.

Site and soil This plant adapts to most soils but prefers soil that is not too loose and does not contain much manure or nitrogenous fertilizer. As a good legume it synthesizes the nitrogen in the air; extra nitrogen promotes excessive leaf growth, to the detriment of flowering and fruiting. Good harvests can be obtained with just the remains of compost from previous crops, but if the soil is very poor, some mature compost can be added. Given the time of year when broad beans are planted, no watering may be necessary, except during a dry spring.

Sowing Sow seeds in open ground in early to mid-autumn in hot regions and in late winter or early spring in cold ones. Sow two to four beans together in holes every 20–25cm/8–10in in rows 45–50cm/18–20in apart.

Care and maintenance When plants are big enough, you can spread a little compost around them, covering it with a straw mulch. Alternatively sow directly in the mulch: the shoots will penetrate the straw. Spring shoots tend to fill up with grey fly or blackfly. These flies may help the flowers to set, so it is worth waiting a few days before removing attacked shoots.

If you leave the best plants unharvested, allowing the pods and beans to dry out, you will have good seeds for next year.

Bean, green (string and flat pole)

Green beans are perhaps the queen of the garden pulses. There are many options, in growth habit and in harvesting, from the early dwarf (string) varieties to the productive climbing (flat pole) beans. There are round beans, flat beans and extra-long beans. Beans also come in different colours, including green, yellow, white and spotted. They can be harvested when young or left until the beans swell up and harvested dry as pulses. Rich nutritionally, especially in proteins, they can be enjoyed in a wide variety of dishes.

Site and soil Green beans like loose, open soil rich in humus. They do not like manured soil, and the presence of any unbroken-down compost in the soil can cause the seeds to rot. They are best grown at the end of a rotation cycle, being the least demanding in terms of soil nutrients. They grow well in what is left in the soil from previous crops. Soil conditions and sowing technique are similar in almost all varieties of bean.

Sowing Sow dwarf beans in holes every 3–5cm/1¼–2in, leaving 15–20cm/6–8in between rows. Tall climbing beans need more space and are usually sown in holes every 7–10cm/3–4in with 60–70cm/24–27in between rows.

Sow in spring (for sowing times, see page 56) when the soil is neither too dry nor too wet. It is better to water the day before sowing than to sow in dry soil and then water, as the seeds have a tendency to rot. Bury seeds 2–3cm/¾–1¼in deep, covering them with fine soil. Sow in bare soil (without a mulch). In cold regions or during a cold spell seeds are usually left to soak in water for twenty-four hours before sowing.

Care and maintenance After sowing, do not water until the shoots have emerged and you can see the first leaves. In humid conditions you might not need to water for a week or two after germination.

Once plants have emerged you need to be attentive and hoe regularly to keep the soil loose, aerated and free of competing weeds. When plants are 25–30cm/10–12in high, you can spread a little worm compost on the soil and mulch with straw to keep weeds down and reduce water needs. If you opt for not applying a mulch, it is a good idea to build up the earth around the stalks. Climbing beans need staking from when the first shoots start reaching upwards. Using bamboo or branches, make supports 2–3m/7–10ft high (or sow next to sweetcorn/corn, up which the beans can climb). In windy weather you can help the bean plants wrap around the supports.

In order for flowers to set properly it is best not to water plants in their first stage of flowering but to wait until the first pods appear. Pick the bean pods young, as soon as they are well formed, and harvest regularly every three or four days. If the beans are left to swell up, the plant stops developing and may shed its flowers (the plant concentrates its energy into making seeds). An exception to this rule is any plant you want to reserve for harvesting as dry beans or for seeds.

Possible problems can appear at the time of sowing and germination, when an excess of humidity in the ground or too much fresh organic matter can damage seeds. Keep an eye out for when the first fragile shoots appear, as they are particularly appetizing to grey worms and slugs and snails. Be ready to take the necessary preventative or mitigating measures.

Another frequent pest in hot periods or climates is red spider mite. Attack is more likely if the ground below the plants is allowed to dry out. Keep it moist with the help of a straw mulch or a layer of old compost.

If you want to eat green beans throughout the growing season (the length depending on region and climate), you need to plan a staggered sowing of dwarf beans every month and a half to two months.

Beetroot

Broccoli

Beetroot is becoming increasingly popular for its many nutritional and therapeutic qualities. There are many varieties, and it is worth trying them all so that you can choose those that grow best in your garden.

Beetroots prefer a soil of average consistency, loose and rich in humus, although they will also tolerate heavy clay soils.

Seeds can be sown directly in the ground from April or in a protected seedbed in February/March. Each `seed´ is in fact a little nest of seeds from which sprout many plants, which may need thinning. Wait until the beetroots are as big as cherries before transplanting. After pulling them up, cut back the leaves and the main root before transplanting outside. Leave 10–15cm/4–6in between plants and some 20–30cm/8–12in between rows.

Beetroot is a moderately demanding plant in terms of nutrients, but normally the remains of compost previously applied (if plenty was applied) are enough. Immature compost or manure makes the beetroot grow too rapidly and develop cracks. Beetroot grows well with celery, cabbages, onions and lettuces, and presents barely any problems as long as it is kept weed free and regularly watered (if the ground is allowed to dry out, the beetroots become hard and crack or break in two when watered again).

Broccoli (also called calabrese) are first cousins of cauliflowers, but have more nutritional qualities. They are reputed to be anticarcinogenic.

They are easy to grow. Their needs in terms of soil, manure, watering and care are similar to those described for cauliflowers (page 64), but they have a slower growth cycle, and they are also a bit hardier: some varieties can survive down to –5°C/23°F. Another difference is in the method of harvesting. Whereas once a cauliflower head is cut the plant is pulled up, with broccoli when the head is cut small flowering shoots grow between the leaves and the central stalk, providing a staggered harvest for several months. For sowing and transplanting times, see page 56.

Brussels sprout

Cabbage, dense-headed and loose-headed

Brussels sprouts are similar to traditional cabbages, differing in that they sprout little cabbages between the leaves and the stalk when they get to about 1m/39in high. Care and maintenance is similar to that of cabbages, with the exception of the amount of manure/compost needed. Brussels sprouts are better grown in soil that does not have too much fresh compost or nitrogen nutrients, as too much nitrogen results in small open sprouts. For sowing and transplanting times, see page 56. When planting, leave 50–60cm/20–24in between plants and 60–70cm/24–27in between rows.

Cabbages, both smooth-leaved and curly-leaved, have been cultivated in Europe for thousands of years (the Romans were great cabbage eaters, believing them to be an antidote for hangovers). Apart from being delicious, they have nutritional and therapeutic qualities that are without comparison.

There is a huge number of varieties, with different shapes, colours and growing cycles. At one extreme are the early cabbages that take only seven weeks and at the other extreme the slow-to-grow but exquisite Lombard cabbages with their characteristic intense purple colour. In much of the Mediterranean cabbages can be grown almost all year round. The exception is winter in regions with heavy frosts and the end of spring/summer in very hot regions, as cabbages have a tendency to bolt easily.

Site and soil Cabbages prefer deep, fertile soils that are not too acidic. The soil should be rich in humus, which makes it better at retaining moisture. Cabbages have no problem with damp climates and like salty sea breezes.

Sowing and transplanting Cultivating cabbages is easy. For sowing times, see page 56. Plant out (in good weather) when plants are 6–10cm/2½–4in high.

Before transplanting, roots can be splashed with clay to which a little whey has been added as a fungicide.

Planting distance is 40–60cm/16–24in between plants and 50–70cm/20–27in between rows, depending on the size reached by the plant.

Care and maintenance A way to use space well that gives good results is to plant the cabbages in a row down the middle of a bed. Either side of the cabbages put lettuces, rocket (arugula), escarole (broad-leaved endive), Swiss chard or celery. Complement the bed with a row of onions planted on the sunny side and a row of leeks planted on the shady side.

Some gardeners companion plant rows of dwarf green beans or peas alternated with the rows of cabbages. The plants′ root systems combine well and the legumes supply additional nitrogen. During the early stages of the cabbages′ growth quick-growing lettuces can be planted between the cabbages.

Once the cabbages are transplanted and well watered, spread 2–4kg/4–9lb of compost on the soil and cover with a good layer of mulch. From now on you need only ensure regular watering until harvest time, perhaps harvesting leaves as you need them to add to a soup or stew. A common problem is aphid attack in spring or in times of heavy rainfall, or when too much nitrogenous fertilizer has been used. Another potential problem is a plague of cabbage caterpillars. You can easily get rid of these manually by destroying the orange nests of eggs on the back of the leaves. Alternatively apply *Bacillus thuringiensis* at dusk (see page 154).

Carrot

The carrot should certainly have a place in your garden. There are many varieties, with different forms, lengths, colours and tastes. As carrots can be sown almost year round, it is best to do staggered sowings, choosing varieties best adapted to the particular season.

Site and soil The best soil for carrots is light, well drained, fertile and stone free. Stones in the ground will cause the carrots to fork, making them more difficult to pull out of the ground. Carrots are intolerant of fresh manure or compost, which causes the growth of lots of little beardy side roots. It is best to grow them in the remains of a previous crop′s compost, after lettuces, for example, or other leaf crops.

Sowing Carrot seeds have a long germination time and need the ground to be moderately warm, so there is no point sowing them too early. In hot regions sow from February on but in cold regions you might need to wait until April.

Seed can be sown in rows (some 10–20cm/4–8in apart) or scattered on the ground and moved lightly around with a rake or with the fingers. The seeds should not be buried and during dry periods will need to be watered morning and evening to stop the top layer of the soil drying out, until plants are 1–2cm/½–¾in high.

If you have difficulty in scattering the seeds evenly, you might find that it helps to mix them with fine sand or old leafmould. Spread the mixture evenly on the soil. Spreading a fine layer of leafmould on the ground that has been sown stops a crust forming and helps the fragile carrots to emerge.

Care and maintenance The biggest bother in growing carrots is that until the seeds have germinated it is not possible to put down a straw mulch, and as germination is very slow the ground tends to get invaded by weeds in the meantime. The most practical solution to this is to carry out one or two 'false sowings' or cover the ground with a dark mesh. The shade cast by the mesh impedes the germination of weed seeds at the same time as warming the earth. It also stops the soil from drying out too fast. After ten to twelve days take away the mesh, leaving the carrots to grow freely and removing by hand the few weeds that might come up.

The only care necessary with carrots is to make sure that they are regularly watered and above all kept weed free. If you have sown densely, you will need to thin well, leaving 3–8cm/1½–3in between plants, depending on variety. If you fail to thin the carrots in time you will end up with a mountain of 'microcarrots', and even if you thin them later the carrots will not thicken and will stay the same size until they flower.

The other problem encountered with carrots is that they cannot take excessive heat or the soil drying out. The latter causes the roots to become hard and the carrots to bolt, hardening the heart of the carrots and making them inedible. Also, periods of drought followed by heavy watering cause the carrots to develop cracks.

Attack by carrot fly, which makes the roots wormy, can be controlled by companion planting. Grow onions in between the carrots or grow onions on the edges of carrot beds.

In soils that are poor in humus and organic matter and where there is little biological activity the carrots can become infested with nematodes. In this case you need to respect long rotation cycles and leave at least four years before growing carrots in the same plot.

Cauliflower

Cauliflowers are cabbages that have been selectively bred to develop large flower heads, which is the part that is eaten.

There are many different types of cauliflower, with different-size heads and even different colours. Although white cauliflowers are the most commonly grown, there are also varieties with purple flower heads, as well as the exotic Romanesco type. Broccoli, although similar to cauliflowers, have different characteristics and growth habit.

Site and soil The growth cycle of cauliflowers is usually long (between four and six months), which means you need to plan sowing and transplanting well when deciding to grow them. In a family garden a practical option is to sow and transplant a few cauliflowers of different varieties every one or two months. This provides a staggered harvest; otherwise you risk being inundated with them all at once.

Cauliflowers do not tolerate hot summers, so in most Mediterranean gardens they can be grown only from autumn until spring. They are very demanding plants in terms of nutrients, so that if there is not already a good reserve left in the soil from previous crops, spread some 3–4kg/7–9lb of well-matured compost per 1m²/11ft².

Cauliflowers like loose, springy soil, rich in humus and compost. Except in times of copious rainfall they need frequent watering.

Sowing and transplanting Sow in protected seedbeds, either in modular trays or in the ground. Prick out into pots when plants have three or four leaves. In order not to have too many cauliflowers at once it is a good idea to select the healthiest looking plants and not bother transplanting any that show signs of weakness or have damaged central stems.

Planting distance varies, depending on how large a particular variety gets and whether the cauliflowers are being grown alone or interspersed with other crops. Common practice is to leave some 60–70cm/24–27in between plants and 70–80cm/27–32in between rows.

Care and maintenance After transplanting, water well at the foot of every plant so that it roots well and spread 3–4kg of mature compost per 1m²/7–11lb per 11ft², covering it all with a good layer of mulch. Comfrey leaf mulch or compost provides a good dose of potassium, which is needed for the formation of the flower heads (wood ash is also a good mineral and potassium provider).

As cauliflowers are nutrient-greedy and impoverish the soil, it is preferable not to grow them in the same place for several years.

An interesting way to grow cauliflowers is along the centre line of beds, planting lettuces or escarole (broad-leaved endive) in rows alongside. You can also grow them with dwarf green beans or peas, which provide them with additional nitrogen.

Celery

For a family three or four celery plants are usually sufficient. If you regularly make celery stock, an excellent blood purifier, you might want to plant more.

Site and soil Celery is a European marsh plant by origin and needs a lot of watering. It grows best in cool, moisture-retentive soils with plenty of organic matter. To ensure good growth, apply 2–4kg/4–9lb of mature compost per 1m²/11ft².

Sowing and transplanting Celery can be sown under glass or directly outside from early spring. You can do an initial pricking out into pots when plants have two or three leaves. When plants have developed more of a root system, they can be transplanted into the garden. Space plants 40–50cm/16–20in apart with 40–50cm/16–20in between rows. It is a good idea to cut back the leaves to prevent dehydration.

Care and maintenance Spread some 2cm/¾in of mature compost on the soil (previously enriched with compost or manure), followed by a deep mulch. In a family garden it does not make much sense to wait until the stalks have reached their maximum thickness to harvest the whole plant. It is more practical to cut leaves as needed (they are delicious as a salad). This way you can be harvesting over a period of months.

Earthing up and blanching is not recommended. It is better that plants receive sunlight and you enjoy the vitamins and minerals in the green chlorophyll.

When plants go to seed in spring or summer they can be pulled up or the flowering stems cut down to allow new leaves to sprout.

Courgette (zucchini)

Cucumber

Courgettes are one of the easiest and most productive vegetables to grow. With three or four plants you have more than enough for a family. There is a wide variety to choose from: long, short, round, flat, green, white, yellow, and more.

Site and soil Courgettes like a well-manured, loose, aerated, humus-rich soil that retains humidity well.

Sowing and transplanting Sow seeds in pots under cover or directly outside from early to late spring. When leaves and roots are well developed, transplant into holes that have had a good dose of mature compost.

Care and maintenance After transplanting spread 3–5kg/7–11lb of compost (it does not need to be well broken down) on the soil, covering it with a good layer of straw mulch. At this early stage of growth keep an eye out for slugs, which can make courgette plants disappear overnight. If slugs are a problem, put plates of beer or iron phosphate granules near by.

If you have given plants enough compost initially and maintained the mulch, you can expect to start harvesting courgettes four to six weeks after planting.

Depending on the variety and climate conditions, harvesting can continue without a break for the next three to five months. Be sure to harvest courgettes young; don't leave them to get big, as when seed production starts the plant is weakened. Cut away any old leaves that show signs of mildew.

The cucumber is a refreshing vegetable that belongs to the plant family known as cucurbits. It climbs wherever it can, either along the ground or up supports – the latter making it possible to grow it in small spaces and making harvesting easier.

There is a great variety of cucumbers, differing in size, length, colour and also flavour.

The cultivation of cucumbers is similar to that of melons (page 71), except that they can be grown closer together – 60 x 90cm/24 x 36in – if trained up frames, and they are a little more resistant to low temperatures. Cucumbers can be sown and transplanted fifteen days to a month before melons (depending on local climate).

Like melons and courgettes, cucumbers grow well with sweetcorn (corn), although this should be sown on the north or east side to avoid the shade it casts, which can cause problems with powdery mildew.

It is advisable to harvest cucumbers before they start to turn yellow, as when they form seeds the plant stops its growth and reduces the formation of new flowers and fruit. Avoid watering with sprinklers; drip irrigation is recommended. In rainy periods it may be necessary to apply treatments of horsetail or whey to prevent powdery mildew proliferating. If plants are badly affected, cut out old and affected leaves.

Escarole (broad-leaved endive)

Fennel

There are many types of escarole that can be grown in the garden, varying from those with fine, indented leaves to the wide, juicy leaf type.

The cultivation of escarole is very similar to that of lettuces (page 70), with the difference that in general escarole are not tolerant of intense heat, so that growing them is restricted to autumn, winter and the beginning of spring.

Sowing and transplanting In hot regions escarole can be sown from August or September through to January. In cold regions they can be sown almost all year round. Sowing and transplanting is as described for lettuces.

Care and maintenance Escarole hearts can be blanched in the same way as lettuces. Leaves can be tied up with string, or a ceramic tile or a big flower pot can be put over the plant.

Cultivated fennel bulbs are first cousins of the fennel that grows wild in many parts of the Mediterranean.

It is a plant selected for the swollen base of its leaves, deliciously succulent in salads and stews or in a béchamel sauce.

The biggest problem in growing fennel in hot climates is its tendency to bolt as soon as it gets hot, before the bulb has swollen. For this reason it is advisable to grow it only in autumn and at the beginning of spring.

Site and soil Fennel is a demanding plant in terms of nutrients and water and likes loose soils that have been well fed with very mature compost.

Sowing It can be sown in seedbeds, in modular trays or directly in the soil in rows 30–40cm/12–16in apart (for sowing times, see page 56). When plants are 5–10cm/2–4 high, or the stalks are a pencil thick, they can be planted out (or transplanted into new rows if they were sown directly). Leave 15–20cm/6–8in between plants.

Care and maintenance Fennel can be grown in bare soil but will need frequent hoeing to remove competing weeds. An interesting alternative is to use a mulch of straw or other organic matter such as shredded prunings.

Garlic

Kohlrabi

Site and soil Garlic does well in light, well-drained soils; avoid planting in heavy waterlogged ground. With the exception of very degraded soils, which should be manured, the remains of compost from previous crops are sufficient for garlic.

Sowing Push the flat base of the garlic clove into the soil, leaving the tip sticking out. It is best to plant during a full or waning moon, as garlic tends to pop out of the soil when the moon is new. Half a kilo/1lb of garlic is enough to plant a row of 6–8m/20–26ft (depending on the size), leaving 6–10cm/2½–4in between cloves. Plant varieties to be eaten young ('spring' garlic) closer together (5cm/2in), as they are harvested while small. In dry areas garlic can be planted from the end of October up until January. In cold, wet regions it is best to plant from January to March.

Maintenance Garlic requires little care and minimal watering. The soil does not need extra manure either before or during growth. Keep an eye out for too much humidity. During rainy or very humid periods it can be a good idea to apply fermented horsetail or a dilution of 5 per cent whey. Garlic is better cultivated in open ground than mulched; hoe regularly to prevent weeds. In wet climates it is a good idea to clear the soil away from the base of the bulbs to facilitate aeration and avoid problems of excess humidity and fungal attack. Traditionally wood ash is sprinkled around garlic plants.

Harvesting Harvest when the bulbs are well formed and the leaves are beginning to dry out.

Kohlrabi is a curious vegetable: while being from the cabbage family (brassica), what in fact is eaten is not the leaf but the swollen stem.

For sowing times see page 56. Otherwise, cultivation and requirements are very similar to those of cabbages (page 62) and cauliflowers (page 64). Kohlrabi, however, have a shorter season, are not attacked by the cabbage caterpillar, and are more drought tolerant.

Given that the plants are smaller than cabbage plants, planting distance is also less, 20 x 30cm/8 x 12in. Being demanding plants in terms of nutrients, they need a rotation of five years before being planted again in the same place.

Lamb's lettuce (corn salad)

Leek

Lamb's lettuce is beginning to be better appreciated as an exquisite and vitamin-rich salad. Conditions needed in terms of site and soil are similar to those of lettuces (page 70) or spinach (page 76). The difference is that it is a plant grown only in autumn/winter, as it does not tolerate heat and bolts rapidly in spring.

Sowing in seedbeds and transplanting is not necessary, as sowing directly in the soil works well as long as soil moisture is maintained. Sow into bare earth in rows 15–20cm/6–8in apart, leaving 0.5–1cm/¼–½in between seeds (that is, more densely than lettuce).

Being low growing, it is ideal for planting under bigger plants such as cabbages, lettuces or leeks, with which it associates well.

Leaves can be harvested as needed or you can wait until the plant is at its maximum development and cut it whole.

Site and soil Leeks like a cool loam rich in humus. Their nutrient needs are moderate and they grow well in the compost left in the soil after previous crops.

Sowing and transplanting For sowing times see page 56. When sowing either in a seedbed or directly in the ground in rows, remember that 3g/0.11 oz of seeds makes a 4m/13ft row and produces 600–800 leeks. The soil or potting compost needs to be kept damp until germination. When the leeks are the thickness of a pencil, pull them up, cut the roots (leaving 1cm/½in of root) and cut one-third of the leaves to prevent dehydration. The dug-up leeks can then be left up to forty-eight hours before being transplanted. The drying-out toughens them against possible leek worm attack.

Care and maintenance In a system of raised beds leeks are usually planted in the sloping edges because of their height. Carrots, which associate well with leeks, can be grown in the flat part of the bed. Plan regular sowings and transplantings, as between sowing and harvesting there are some five or six months. Planting distance depends on the final thickness of the leeks, the variety chosen and the climate, but there should be 6–10cm/2½–4in between leeks and at least 25–35cm/10–15in between rows. Planting depth is 10cm/4in; a pencil or stick can be used to make the holes. Give the plants a good watering immediately after transplanting to help them root well.

In organic gardens leeks do not tend to have problems with pests.

Lettuce

For most of the year a great variety of lettuces can be grown in practically any garden and in very different climate zones. In colder regions you may need to protect lettuces with plastic tunnels or grow them in mini greenhouses. In hot regions from early spring onwards only those varieties resistant to bolting, such as 'Summer Wonder', should be sown or transplanted.

Site and soil Lettuces grow well in fertile, humus-rich soils that retain moisture. In summer it is worth growing them in semi-shaded places to avoid early bolting. As the growing cycle is short, lettuces can be grown in between slower-growing plants such as tomatoes, peppers, aubergines (eggplants) or cabbages. When the tomatoes or cabbages are starting to get big and need more space, it will already be time to harvest the lettuces.

Lettuces are moderately demanding in terms of nutrients. If the previous crop was well manured, they do not need anything extra. Where the soil is poor, 2–3kg/4–7lb of mature compost per 1m^2/11ft^2 can be added.

Sowing and transplanting Lettuces can be sown directly outside from March to September in most regions and in seedbeds the rest of the year, protected from cold when necessary. When plants are 6–8cm/2½–3¼in, prick out into recycled containers or pots; when they have rooted well and are some 10cm/4in high, transplant outside Leave 10–30cm/

10–12in between lettuces and 40–60cm/16–24in between rows, spacing depending on variety and growing method.

It is important to plan sowing and transplanting well in order to be able to harvest lettuces daily. Sow at least once a month and transplant regularly. Transplanting twenty lettuces, preferably of different varieties, every fifteen days will provide you with a healthy salad daily.

Care and maintenance If lettuces are grown in beds or strips with a good top dressing of compost, a straw mulch and a system of drip irrigation, no more attention is required other than overseeing the irrigation and the control of aphids in critical periods. If, on the other hand, they are grown in furrows in bare earth they will need continual weeding and more copious watering to allow for greater evaporation from the soil in hot periods.

Possible problems Too much fresh compost and nitrogenous fertilizers can cause problems with aphids. Excessive watering and humidity favours putrefaction and slug attack. Too little watering causes water stress and leads to weak growth with yellow, fibrous, bitter leaves and a tendency to bolt.

Crisphead lettuce varieties such as 'Iceberg' or 'Summer Wonder' do not require blanching, but others such as Romaine (cos) lettuce may need tying with a piece of string or a rubber band to make the inner leaves more tender (although green leaves, which are richer in chlorophyll, are always healthier).

Harvesting Harvesting normally consists of cutting the whole lettuce when it has reached full size and before it bolts and goes to seed. However, you can also harvest just the outside leaves, as with Swiss chard (page 78), when the lettuce is half formed (about 15cm/6in in diameter). By picking an outside leaf from every lettuce you can have a salad every day, prolonging by more than a month the harvest period. You will also be eating the leaves richest in chlorophyll, nutrients and minerals.

Melon

Melons are fruits that are frequently grown in the vegetable garden. The melon has come to us from the hot regions of Asia. While it has adapted and grows very well in Mediterranean gardens, as it is a sun-lover the flowers can have difficulty setting or the fruit maturing in colder or more humid regions.

Site and soil If possible cultivate melons in the sunniest part of the garden in loose, fertile soil. Put a couple of spadefuls of very mature compost in each hole where the melon is to be sown or transplanted.

Sowing and transplanting Melon seeds can be sown directly outside from March or April or a little earlier in a protected seedbed. If sowing in a seedbed,

it is best to sow in little pots to make it easier to transplant without harming the roots. If sowing directly outside, mix the soil with sieved, very mature compost. Sow four or five seeds per hole, leaving 70–80cm/27–32in between holes and at least 1m between rows. When the plants start appearing, pull up the weakest or least healthy-looking plants until only one plant is left per hole. In cold regions plants can be protected in this early phase with a plastic cover or using plastic water containers. In the germination stage it is a good idea to deter snails and slugs by putting circles of wood ash around each plant, or beer traps, or iron phosphate granules.

Care and maintenance If growing in bare soil, you need to hoe weekly to keep weeds under control and aerate the soil. Ideally, when the plants have four to six leaves, spread a layer of compost on the ground (3–5kg/7–11lb per 1m²/11ft²) and mulch with straw or other organic leftovers.

In regions that are climatically less favourable to melon growing, pruning the plants can be a great help. In the first phase of pruning cut the central stalk, leaving two or three lateral vines. After the flowers have set, pinch out the tips of the lateral vines. In the third phase, when the melons are formed, cut back the rest of the vines to three or four leaves above each well-formed melon. It is best not to leave more than three or four melons per plant, as more will not have a chance to mature and ripen.

Apart from possible attack by aphids or thrips, both relatively easy to control, powdery mildew can be a problem in the leaves. Try not to wet the leaves when watering (drip irrigation is best) and if necessary treat with horsetail or whey.

Melons grow well with sweetcorn (corn). The sweetcorn can be sown alongside the melons 60–70cm/24–27in apart, protecting the melon plants from dominant winds or intense sun, depending on local climate.

Harvesting You can tell when a melon is ripe by its colour and aroma. Other signs are when the little leaf stuck to the melon dries, or when the stalk has started to separate, or when the flowering end of the melon gives way easily when pressed.

71

Onion

There are numerous varieties of onion with shorter or longer growing cycles. Some varieties are to be eaten fresh, while others are for drying and can be kept for months. They can be round, long, small, flattened, large, white, red, etc. By growing a combination of varieties according to taste and the time of year you can have fresh or dried onions almost all year round.

Site and soil Onions like a light, cool, aerated soil rich in humus. They do not do well in heavy, wet soil. In terms of manure/compost they are very undemanding plants and can be planted in the third stage of a rotation cycle, i.e. after two cycles of more nutrient-demanding crops in the same plot. Plant, for example, after lettuces, spinach or escarole (broad-leaved endive). In a bed system onions are usually planted on the sloping edges of the bed, as they do not need much water and this maximizes the use of space.

Sowing and transplanting Seeds can be sown most of the year. Usually they are sown in an open seedbed from August to September for winter transplanting and spring harvesting or sown under cover from January to March for harvesting at the end of summer and in autumn.

Depending on variety, transplant onions 10–20cm/4–8in apart with 25–30cm/10–12in between rows. When transplanting it is important to cut back the roots of the small plants to 1–2cm/½–¾in from the base to ensure better root growth and better bulb development later. In hot periods it is advisable to cut back the leaves by a third.

Care and maintenance Onions are hardy plants needing little care. Maintenance consists solely of controlling competitive weeds, by either mulching or regular hoeing. When the bulb is fully formed, bend the stalk to prevent the plant bolting and going to seed. Onions that are for storage should be harvested when two-thirds of the leaves show signs of drying. Leave them spread out on the ground for a few days or on top of a wood pallet to dry before storing.

Onions to be eaten fresh can be harvested as needed.

Parsley

Pea

Parsley is a good garden companion, worth having to hand for its numerous culinary uses.

Site and soil It likes cool, loose soil rich in humus. It does not grow well in clay or very acidic soil; nor does it tolerate immature compost or manure.

Sowing and transplanting Parsley can be sown in a seedbed or directly in the ground from the end of February or in March (April in cold regions). As it tends to bolt in summer, sow again at the end of August for a winter supply. Four or five parsley plants are normally enough for a family garden; more can be planted between other crops such as cabbages or tomatoes or with aromatic and medicinal plants. If you are parsley lovers and want a bigger supply, scatter seeds or sow in rows, thinning to 4–6cm/1½–2½in between plants.

Care and maintenance Parsley is a hardy plant and requires no more than a little weeding and regular watering and cutting. Cut regularly, even when the leaves are not required, so that young tender leaves keep coming and flowering is delayed.

There are many varieties of peas suitable for a family garden, from dwarf varieties to mangetout, which need staking. Apart from being nutritious, peas enrich the soil with nitrogen and improve soil structure.

Site and soil Peas adapt to almost any soil but do better in damp, lightish soil. They dislike flooding and excessive dryness. They absorb atmospheric nitrogen and do not need much manure, growing well in what is left in the soil from previous crops. If soil is poor, 2–3kg/4–7lb of well-rotted manure can be laid around the plants when they are 6–10cm/2½–4in high.

Sowing Peas are grown in autumn and spring, as they deal better with cold than with summer heat, which can cause fungal problems. Sow from late September to December or in cold soils and climates from February to April. In open ground sow three or four seeds together in holes every 25cm/10in in rows 40–60cm/16–24in apart. Some gardeners sow a single seed every 1–2cm/½–¾in, with good results. Climbing peas, being bigger plants, need wider spacing.

Care and maintenance Hoe to keep the soil free of weeds. When plants are 10–15cm/4–6in high some mature compost can be laid on the soil. Cover it with a straw mulch. Make a frame out of bamboo canes or branches to support climbing peas. Watering should be light. From sowing to harvest takes two to three months, depending on variety. To prolong the harvest, pick regularly as soon as pods have swelled up.

Pepper

Sweet peppers and their fellow capsicums, such as chilli peppers, are solanaceae and come from the semitropical zones of America. They need a lot of sun and high temperatures to grow well and produce a good harvest. This needs to be taken into account when deciding where in the garden to plant them. There are numerous varieties of peppers, with very different flavours, sizes and culinary uses. In the same bed you can plant some four or six plants, each a different classic variety such as sweet red pepper, four-sided pepper, yellow pepper and the long, soft-skinned Italian pepper.

Site and soil Peppers, like tomatoes and aubergines (eggplants), thrive in a fertile, loose, well-dug soil rich in humus. They prefer cool, deep, friable soil and suffer if put in damp, clay, compacted ground. Being greedy plants, they need a good amount of compost, some 3–5kg/7–11lb per 1m²/11ft². This is better left on the surface than dug in.

Sowing and transplanting The cultivation of peppers is very similar to that of tomatoes (page 79) and aubergines (page 59). The difference is that peppers need more sunlight and heat than tomatoes and are therefore sown and planted out a month later.

Care and maintenance As with tomatoes, the best way to grow peppers is in soil covered with compost and a mulch. Some gardeners wait until the beginning of June to put down the mulch. This gives the soil a chance to warm up so that the plants develop faster. In heavy, damp soils it may be a good idea to grow the plants at the top of well-aerated ridges. This is to prevent the stalks rotting and the roots becoming asphyxiated.

Plant a basil plant every four or five peppers as a preventative measure against aphids.

Pepper plants do not generally need staking except in very windy areas; nor do they need pruning except in cold regions. Pruning consists of pinching out the ends of the main shoots at the end of summer so that peppers that are already formed have a better chance of getting big and ripe before the first onset of autumn cold.

Potato

Growing potatoes organically is quite easy, but you do need a fair amount of space. To provide enough for a family's average consumption you need about 30–50m²/323–538ft². If you can do two sowings a year, some 20m²/215ft² will be enough.

Potatoes are originally from the Andes mountains and prefer mild, humid climates that do not get too hot. However, they adapt to all climates and, although affected by frost, if mulched with straw they manage to sprout and complete their cycle.

Site and soil Potatoes like loose, humus-rich soil that has been well dug and manured. The tubers of the potatoes act as nutrient banks, and to swell up and reach a good size they need soil that has been well fed with compost. Spread 4–6kg/9–13lb of compost per 1m²/11ft²; potatoes can tolerate semi-mature compost. Burying basil leaves (fresh or dry) in the soil with the potatoes can considerably increase the size of the potatoes and the quantity harvested.

Sowing/planting In hot and temperate regions potatoes are planted twice a year: once in late winter and once in summer for a late harvest. In cold regions potatoes are planted once a year, in spring, when the risk of frost is past. The most common method of sowing is to cut each potato into a few pieces, each containing at least one bud or sprout. These are buried in well-dug soil, leaving 30–40cm/12–16in between potatoes and 50–70cm/20–27in between rows.

Traditionally the pieces of potato are buried about 6cm/2½in deep in furrows. A simpler way is to place them in rows on levelled earth and cover them with 3–4cm/1¼–1½in of compost. Above this install drip irrigation lines and cover the lot with 4–6cm/1½–2½in of straw. The potato sprouts easily penetrate the compost and straw, and the tubers swell up nicely, practically at ground level, without being weighed down with soil.

The best time for sowing potatoes is during a waning, descending moon.

Care and maintenance Using the latter method (covering the potatoes with compost and straw) there is barely anything to do until harvest time. Water the plants when rainfall is scarce and look out for potato beetle, although this is rarely a problem with organically grown potatoes. Harvesting is made simple by the potatoes being in the compost layer at ground level. The straw mulch, besides stopping weeds, if deep enough also protects the potatoes from sunlight, which turns them green. If you grow in furrows, you need to hoe regularly to remove weeds and earth up the base of the potato plants a couple of times so that the soil stays loose and the potatoes do not turn green.

Downy mildew can occur when humidity is high. A good remedy is to alternate a concoction of horsetail with applications of diluted whey.

Harvesting Harvest the potatoes when the plants start to wither and dry up (normally after flowering). Try digging up one plant to check if the potatoes are fully formed, rubbing the skin with a finger to see how easily it comes off. You might like to harvest some early for immediate consumption as new potatoes.

Harvesting potatoes for long-term storage is best done during a full moon. Harvest during a dry period and leave the potatoes to dry outside for a few hours, protected from the sun by the pulled-up plants. Harvesting mulched potatoes is easy: pull up the plants, draw back the mulch and collect the potatoes, which will be practically on the surface.

Saving potatoes for seed With good organic gardening practices, and so long as you live in an area where there are few aphids, you can try keeping your own potatoes for sowing.

Radish

A space in the garden can always be found for the humble radish, with its peppery flavour, wealth of vitamins and digestive properties. There is a wide range to choose from, from the small red or red and white radishes to the enormous, succulent Majorcan variety, not forgetting the therapeutic black radishes from Japan.

Site and soil Radishes adapt to any soil but prefer one that is light, cool and friable with plenty of humus. They do not tolerate fresh compost or big amounts of manure, which cause them to go hollow and have a hotter flavour. They do best in plots where there is some compost left over from previous crops.

Sowing Except where there are hard frosts. radishes can be sown practically all year round. They are fast growers (six weeks to two months between sowing and harvest), so sow a few seeds every fortnight. That way you have regular harvests and can try out different types. Scatter seeds directly on ground that has been raked to a fine tilth, in rows 10–15cm/4–6in apart, covering the seeds lightly with soil.

Care and maintenance Just keep the area free of weeds and thin to 4–6cm/1½–2½in between radishes.

Watch out for slugs and snails in the first stages of germination and growth. In the event of attack by flea beetles use liquidized garlic and chilli or a natural insecticide. Pull up radishes that have gone to seed as soon as possible and put them on the compost heap, leaving those you wish to keep for seed.

Spinach

This nutritious crop is preferably grown in autumn and spring in most of the Mediterranean, with the exception of cold regions, where it is grown from spring to autumn. This is because of its intolerance of the high temperatures reached in summer and its tendency to bolt as soon as temperatures rise. However, by careful selection from the many varieties available it is possible to cultivate spinach almost all year round.

Site and soil Spinach prefers cool, aerated soils that are rich in humus. It grows well in what is left of compost from previous crops. Although extra feeding is not necessary, a thin layer of worm compost after sowing improves growth.

Sowing It is a good idea to rake and smooth down the soil before sowing. Scatter the seeds or sow in rows some 20–30cm/8–12in apart, depending on the ultimate size of the chosen variety.

Cultivation Ten to fifteen days after germination it is advisable to do a preliminary thinning, leaving 4–8cm/1½–3¼in between plants. When the plants are big enough you can start cutting the largest leaves (as with Swiss chard) and continue harvesting for a month or two. Alternatively you can wait until the plants have reached their maximum growth and then cut them at the root, thus harvesting only once. In Europe it is common practice to scatter seeds in empty plots in autumn as a green manure (3g/0.11oz of seeds per $10m^2/108ft^2$).When the plants flower and go to seed, they are cut down and left in place as a mulch.

Squash

Strawberry

Squash are worth growing in any spare space in the garden. Once harvested, in summer or at the beginning of autumn, they can be kept for months and used to make nutritious soups and purées or baked in the oven.

Their cultivation is almost the same as for courgettes (zucchini) (page 66) or melons (page 71). The difference is in the planting distance, which depends on the growth reached by the particular variety.

A practical place to grow squash is in the borders of the garden, in little-used corners or climbing up fences or piles of brushwood, or where old compost heaps once stood.

Strawberries, perhaps the sweetest and tastiest of all garden crops, grow well in any corner of the garden.

Site and soil Strawberries originate from cool, humid undergrowth and like mildly acidic soil. Grow them in a sunny but cool spot, forking over soil to which has been added well-rotted manure or compost, to maintain acidity and provide food for these greedy plants. Excellent results can be obtained by growing them with 3–5kg/7–11lb of mature compost per 1m²/11ft² under a permanent straw mulch. Add a little worm compost or leafmould at fruiting time, to avoid any shortage of nutrients at the reproductive phase.

Sowing and transplanting Strawberries are best propagated by division or from runners. Runners pulled up in late summer and planted in pots filled with potting compost should root readily. Remove any flowers or fruit. Plant out well-rooted specimens when the danger of frost has passed. Propagating by division can be done in autumn: part of the main plant is dug up, leaving the other part in the soil. If you add a generous layer of compost every winter you can grow strawberries in the same plot for three to four years.

Care and maintenance Strawberries need no special care apart from regular watering, renewing plants and removing runners. Mulching with pine needles, which are more acidic than straw, gives good results, as does sowing garlic or leek between the plants. The greed shown by snails and slugs can make it necessary to resort to beer traps or iron phosphate granules.

Sweetcorn (corn)

Swiss chard

There are many varieties of corn for the garden but unless you have chickens or make semolina, you will only be interested in growing succulent sweetcorn.

Site and soil Sweetcorn is very greedy for water and nutrients. It needs well-manured, humus-rich soil.

Sowing Sweetcorn is sown directly outdoors from early spring onwards. Sow two or three grains at a time in holes or push them into the ground with your fingers. Space 25–30cm/10–12in apart in rows 50–60cm/ 20–24in apart (depending on the ultimate height of the variety). Growing green beans, squash or courgettes (zucchini) with sweetcorn gives excellent results and makes good use of the ground and nutrients.

Care and maintenance When plants are 5–6cm/2–2½in high, select the healthiest ones. Leave these to grow and pull out the rest. Grow corn plants together so that the wind can carry the pollen from flower to flower.

When the sweetcorn is 6–10cm/2½–4in high, you can sow two or three climbing bean seeds at the foot of each plant and thus make use of the sweetcorn plants as a frame for the beans to grow up. When the sweetcorn is 20cm/8in high, spread some mature compost on the ground and cover it with a 5–6cm/2–2½in mulch of straw or other dry plants. If you opt not to mulch, you will need to hoe and weed regularly.

Harvesting The corn is harvested three or four months after sowing. To see if the corn is ready, press the cob with a fingernail, or unwrap the leaves from one cob to see if the grains are ripe.

The visual impact of this humble vegetable is on a par with the ease with which it is grown and the generosity of its production. Swiss chard is a close cousin of beetroot (the seeds are identical) and has the same needs in terms of cultivation. There are many varieties: the stalks can be wide or narrow, red or white, and the leaves may be dark green, light green or curly. It is a plant native to the Mediterranean basin and easily reverts to the wild. Four or five plants are plenty for a family's needs.

Site and soil Swiss chard adapts to any climate, but it does better with regular humidity and dislikes long periods of drought or frost. In raw climates protect it against frost by covering it with straw in winter or earthing up around the stalks until the good weather comes. It prefers clay soils but adapts well to any soil as long as it is cool, loosened to a good depth and rich in humus. As the harvesting period can last more than six months, it is a good idea to add mature compost after every harvest or add new layers of organic matter if using a permanent mulch. The more compost the plant receives, the bigger its leaves will be.

Sowing and transplanting Swiss chard can be sown in a seedbed and pricked out into pots or transplanted bare rooted into the ground when plants are 6–8cm/2½–3¼in high. Leaves can be cut at the moment of transplanting to prevent dehydration. Alternatively, in hot climates or during warm weather sow directly in the ground. Sow two or three seeds together and later thin seedlings, leaving only one plant. Sow and transplant when the moon is waxing.

Care and maintenance Swiss chard only needs to be kept free of weeds; applying a straw mulch both stops weeds and helps retain soil humidity. Being a juicy plant it needs to be kept well watered but not flooded. Watch out for slugs and snails during the first days after transplanting and protect from attack by birds (which love the young leaves) by putting up tape, mirrors or plastic netting.

Harvesting Harvest leaves as they reach a good size. Outside leaves should be cut back regularly anyway to promote better growth in new leaves. As Swiss chard normally flowers in the second year, a staggered harvest can be prolonged from 100 to 200 days, depending on climate. At the end of its cycle or with the arrival of severe cold the plant can be cut down.

Tomato

The tomato is the king of the summer harvest. There are innumerable varieties, including new types coming on the market every year as well as all the local varieties, products of hybridization by cross-pollination. It is worth experimenting and growing different varieties until you find the best ones in terms of taste and culinary use. However, the most important thing is how well they adapt to your climate and soil and their resistance to pests, heat or the ambient humidity (which can cause downy mildew).

Site and soil Tomatoes, although they might not seem it, are robust, vigorous plants that adapt to almost all soils and ambient conditions. However, they are nutrient-greedy and do better in loose, humus-rich soils that have received plenty of compost or manure.

If possible, use drip irrigation and ideally grow the tomatoes in beds that have previously been covered in compost (4–6kg/9–13lb per 1m²/11ft²). If you have comfrey in the garden, put a good layer of comfrey leaves on top of the compost to help the formation of the fruit (comfrey is rich in potassium).

It is also recommended that you grow tomatoes in plots that have been sown the previous autumn/winter with a green manure. Chop up the green manure a month or two before transplanting the tomatoes.

Sowing and transplanting Early sowings (from January to the middle of March) are delicate, as tomatoes do not tolerate frosts and need to be sown in protected seedbeds (or in heated ones in cold regions).

79

When the plants are some 15cm/6in high and have four leaves or more they can be transplanted into pots. It is a good idea to leave potted plants outside for two or three weeks, protecting them at night, so that they harden off and develop good roots.

When the weather is favourable they can be transplanted outside; protect them against cold with plastic 5-litre water containers or with tiles if in a windy area.

Planting distance is 40–50cm/16–20cm between plants and 60–70cm/24–27in between rows. When transplanting, bury the stalk in the ground up to the first leaves to promote root development. If the stalks are very long they can be bent in a curve, with soil covering the curve.

After transplanting, water copiously to ensure good rooting.

Care and maintenance After transplanting, cover the compost and comfrey leaves with a straw mulch, 5–7cm/2–3in thick. This saves both regular weeding and having to earth up the plants. It also creates ideal conditions of humidity and bacterial life, thus providing nutrients throughout the growing cycle so that the tomatoes develop well and give plenty of fruit. With the exception of some varieties of bush tomato, the majority of tomato plants need staking with canes or branches 2–3m/7–10ft long. As the tomato plant grows, nip out most side shoots, leaving the central stem with its bunches of flowers and tomatoes. Tie these to the supports with string or plastic-covered wire (the latter is much quicker to use, only needing twisting; at the end of the season it can be untwisted and kept to be used again).

Side or basal shoots of 6–8cm/2½–3¼in can be planted in pots of potting compost or, in summer, directly in the ground, with the bottom half of the cutting buried in the soil. If watered regularly, they will root well and make new tomato plants.

Once plants have three bunches of flowers, you can start pruning back old leaves at the bottom part of the plant. This helps light to penetrate and the tomatoes mature, at the same time as preventing fungal and other diseases.

Tomatoes are very susceptible to downy mildew, especially in rainy regions or seasons. A preventative treatment of horsetail is advisable. If you notice grey patches, characteristic of mildew, apply diluted whey (0.5 litre/1 pint whey to 10 litres/2½ gallons of water). When tomatoes are grown organically, aphids are rarely a problem, as long as fresh compost or manure has not been dug in at the level of the roots. There might be some aphids from time to time, but they are unlikely to become a plague and if necessary they can be easily controlled with potassium soap or garlic. Planting basil between the tomato plants is also a good way to keep aphids away.

In cold regions from September onwards the growing points of the main stalk can be cut back to help the remaining tomatoes mature.

If you want to save seeds from your favourite or most productive tomatoes, the different varieties need to be planted as far away from each other as possible to avoid hybridization.

Turnip

The cultivation of turnips deserves a revival, given their many culinary uses and therapeutic qualities. Try out different varieties (white, purple, violet, yellow, round, long, short, flat) until you find one that pleases your palette.

Site and soil Turnips are grown in bare soil that has been raked and smoothed down.

Sowing Turnips do not like heat or drought, so are best sown in spring and autumn (or winter in hot regions). If sowing in summer, choose a cool, shady spot. Scatter seed or sow in rows 25–30cm/10–12in apart and cover lightly with soil. Thin plants when 3–6cm/1¼–2½in high, leaving 10–15cm/4–6in between plants.

As turnips are brassicas, like cabbages, they grow well with tomatoes, carrots or lettuces. Turnip seeds can be scattered between these crops and harvested when they reach an adequate size, freeing up the space.

Watermelon

Watermelons are first cousins of melons (page 71) and squashes (page 77) and have the same needs in terms of climate, compost, irrigation, sowing, transplanting and other cultivation techniques.

Because of the size reached by the plants, planting distance is 1 x 1m/39 x 39in. As with melons, the ends of the shoots need to be pinched out once the fruit has begun to swell.

It is a good idea to try to get seeds of local varieties particular to the village or region.

Like melons and squashes, watermelons grow well with compost and mulch and a system of drip irrigation. The latter avoids problems of powdery mildew in the leaves.

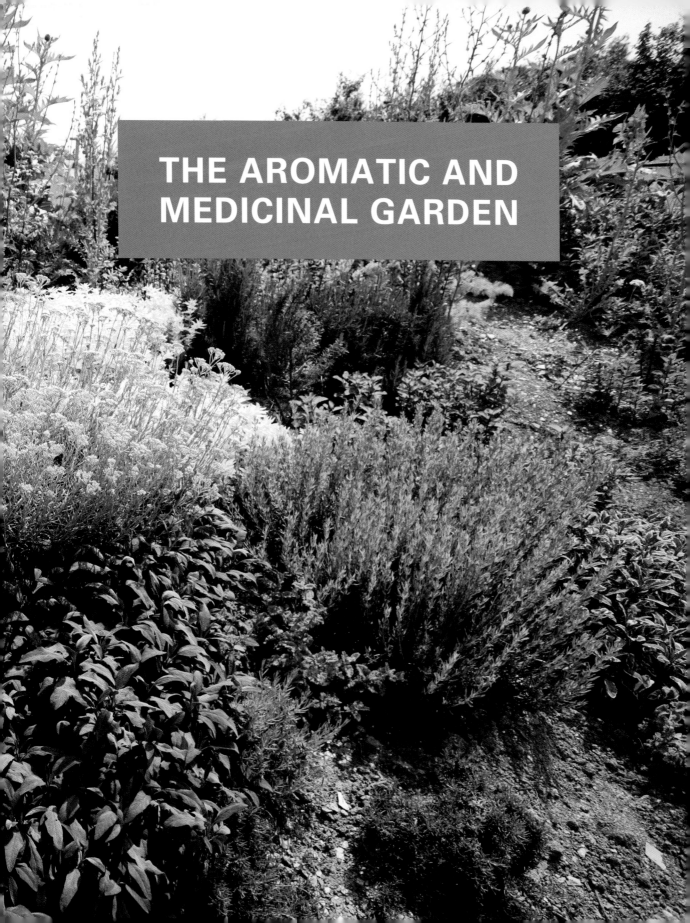

THE AROMATIC AND
MEDICINAL GARDEN

CREATING AN AROMATIC AND MEDICINAL GARDEN

Therapeutic plants

For thousands of years humans have used plants as medicine. Methodical observation, experimentation and oral and written records have enabled the identification and selection of medicinal plants. Despite attempts by commercially motivated interests to stigmatize herbalist practice as being based on superstition, the use of plants as medicine has continued in almost all cultures and on all continents. To this day most active ingredients in modern medicines are obtained directly or indirectly from plants. Growing your own medicinal plants provides you with a magnificent way of encouraging health and vitality. It offers the possibility of having to hand simple, effective, natural remedies with no side effects, with which to treat the majority of common ailments.

Traditionally family gardens contained numerous plants that furnished effective, cheap, homemade remedies. Luckily such uses and all the centuries of wisdom and experience that have gone into them were never entirely lost. Nowadays there is a resurgence of interest in growing medicinal plants and using them to make natural remedies. It would be laudable to follow the steps taken by some eastern countries such as Thailand, Vietnam, Bangladesh or the island of Madagascar, where there are incentives for families to grow the plants necessary for homemade remedies next to their houses. In the family garden you have the chance to put this recommendation into practice and make your own medicinal garden.

For the most part the active ingredients in medicinal plants are the essential oils stored in the tissue of the plant. These are used by the plant to protect it from threats in the environment and so are found in higher concentrations in plants growing wild and in adverse conditions than in cultivated plants.

An attractive mixture of medicinal and aromatic plants.

Boosting biodiversity

If your aim is to have a healthy, productive organic garden, you should do everything possible to create a space that hosts maximum biodiversity. You should try to have your vegetable crops alongside, and in close symbiotic relation with, a variety of aromatic, medicinal and ornamental plants and herbs. There is no need for a garden to be all monotonous straight rows. In fact, gardens that integrate fruit trees, bushes, aromatic plants and herbs as well as self-propagated wild plants make the best use of the space and give the biggest harvests per square metre.

Having a good variety of wild plants, especially aromatic and medicinal ones, is not only for the pleasure to be had in looking at them or smelling them. Such plants also create favourable conditions for pollinating insects and the insect predators of certain pests. Their smell also repels many pests and diseases.

Herbs grown with vegetables and ornamental plants.

Siting the garden and choosing plants

If you do not have the space to create a garden of medicinal and aromatic plants, you can still grow a few herbs such as basil, chives, celery or parsley, interplanted among your tomatoes or lettuces. However, the ideal would be to create hedges consisting of medicinal and aromatic plants and have these around the whole garden, making a beautiful, aromatic, protective barrier. These hedges can be made up of plants as varied as sage, rosemary, thyme, nasturtium, bay, comfrey, marjoram, mint, tansy, camomile, aloe vera, lavender, savory, French marigold, calendula (pot marigold) or valerian, all growing in positive synergy. Such a hedge surrounding the vegetable garden provides an excellent living barrier against wind and any contamination that might waft over from chemical treatments used by neighbours less respectful of the environment and everyone´s health.

A raised bed for drought-tolerant herbs.

Another great advantage of most medicinal and aromatic plants is that they are easy to grow. Most of them are hardy plants and so need little looking after or feeding or watering.

Choose which plants to grow according to your own preference and what is possible, but also pay attention to plant combinations and good synergy with the rest of the plants in the garden. Although it is possible to experiment intuitively, it is worth gathering as much information as possible. A good book on growing aromatic and medicinal plants helps to orientate you as you take your first steps.

You can start by growing the most popular and well-known plants, such as mint, basil, calendula, French marigold, aloe, lavender, rosemary or thyme – all of them easy to find in plant nurseries. Then, little by little, you can start introducing local wild plants and especially useful though less well-known plants such as stevia (which besides being fifty times sweeter than sugar helps to control diabetes). Another very beneficial plant is echinacea, which reinforces the immune system and boosts the body's defences against cold and damp weather.

You can make use of any unused space in the garden to plant medicinal plants: boundaries, below trees, or in pots on the terrace or balcony. Annuals such as French marigold, basil or calendula can be grown between crops.

Designing the garden

Make a plan of your garden showing the characteristics of each space (light/shade, dryness/humidity, fertile/poor soil, closeness to trees, etc.). Using this as a guide, you can create specific areas with different ecosystems: for example, a dry area with rocks and pebbles, places with deeper, more fertile soil and a well-watered, more humid area. Then make a plan, distributing plants according to where they will grow best.

Another possibility is a herb spiral made by building a spiralling wall with stone or wooden stakes so that the centre of the spiral is the highest point and the outside of the spiral the lowest point. The base of the spiral need be only about 1.5–2m/5–7ft wide, making it a good option if space is limited. Build up the soil to the level of the walls of the spiral and plant it up. At the top, where it will be driest, put oil-rich plants such as rosemary, and at the bottom, where there will be more humidity, plant herbs such as parsley. The herb spiral, with its efficient use of space through stacking plants vertically and the creation of different conditions for different plants, is a beautiful illustration of permaculture.

If you are fortunate enough to have water passing through the garden – a natural stream or biologically recycled water from a septic tank – you can make a little pond or lagoon. This can be planted with aquatic plants and stocked with fish. As well as adding to the biodiversity of your garden, it will improve the microclimate and stimulate all garden life.

Young gardeners creating a herb spiral.

Aloe vera

Angelica

Aloe vera is both ornamental and rich in medicinal properties. There are many varieties of aloe but aloe vera contains the most active ingredients. It is easily differentiated by its larger, fleshier, paler green leaves and will thrive in a spot where it can stay for years (although it also transplants well). It is worth having close by the house, ready for when it is needed to alleviate sunburn, regenerate badly treated skin or heal wounds. The gel can be liquidized with other fruit or vegetables and taken as a drink to treat digestive or ulcerous disorders.

Aloes grow well in almost all soils but do not tolerate intense cold or frosts, and in regions with cold winters will need to be planted in pots and brought in for the winter. Too much water can cause rotting.

They are easy to propagate from the 'baby' aloes that sprout next to plants that are more than two years old. You can buy your first aloe in a nursery or garden centre and then propagate more plants.

Angelica is a hardy biennial rich in minerals, vitamins and antioxidants whose leaves can be eaten raw in salad. It likes deep, fertile, humus-rich soil and needs space, as it grows to a good size. It can be grown from seed sown in autumn.

Adapting the dates for your region
In the following pages, dates for sowing times refer to a temperate Mediterranean climate with mild winters and summers that are not too hot. For how to adapt dates for other regions, see page 56.

Anise

Basil

Green anise is one of the best plants for digestion and for relieving flatulence. It is a generally hardy annual that likes a hot, dry climate and should be planted in a sunny well-drained spot. Propagation and cultivation is similar to that of fennel (page 67). The flowers can be wrapped in mosquito net and harvested when they turn dark brown. Hang the flower heads under shelter to finish drying.

Basil is one of the most popular garden annuals, with many aromatic and culinary uses. It is also very useful in the garden, as it both protects other crops and stimulates them to greater and better quality production. It likes deep, loamy, humus-rich, fertile soil and although it can tolerate drought it grows more prolifically if given plenty of water and the soil stays damp. It needs a sunny spot in the garden and it is common to plant it next to peppers and tomatoes, as it protects them from aphid attack.

Basil is sensitive to cold and frosts. It can be sown in a protected seedbed in early spring. Choose from among the many varieties available: wide- or narrow-leaved, green, violet, orange, mentholated, tasting of pineapple, of lemon . . . the list goes on.

When plants are 5–6cm/2–2½in high, transplant them into big pots or directly into the ground, either in the medicinal garden or between crops to be protected. Leaves can be picked as soon as they are established and used for cooking or mixed with the soil where potatoes are to be sown to increase the harvest.

Bay (sweet bay)

Bay is a bush that over the years can grow into a big tree. Unless you are prepared to prune it regularly, it is only feasible to grow it if you have a lot of space.

It can be grown from cuttings in July and August, from seed and also by layering. It adapts to all soils and climates but does not tolerate temperatures below −10°C/14°F.

Borage

In some regions borage is grown as a vegetable and its leaves and stalks are eaten in soups or fried in batter. It is a hardy annual that grows well in any garden soil though it prefers one that has been well manured and drains well. It likes sun but also grows well in semi-shade. It needs regular watering for the stalks to swell up for use in soups. It can be sown in a protected seedbed at the end of winter or directly outside in early spring for harvesting at the end of spring and early summer; or it can be sown from August to September for harvesting in autumn or winter. The flowers can also be harvested and dried for use in infusions for treating respiratory problems.

Calendula (pot marigold)

Camomile

The majesty of its yellow and orange flowers, blooming throughout the year in some regions, together with its medicinal and culinary properties, make calendula one of the garden's and the gardener's best friends. Its petals are exquisite raw in salad and the flowers can be used to make the well-known calendula cream. This cream is one of the best treatments for minor lesions and skin problems such as eczema.

Calendula is an annual (sometimes biennial) plant that adapts to almost all soils and climates. It tolerates both drought and frost but it prefers a well-drained soil and a hot climate. It is easy to grow from seed and will spread by self-seeding. Sow directly outside in early spring in temperate zones or in late spring in colder climates. It can also be sown in a protected seedbed from February.

German camomile (*Matricaria recutita*) is an annual plant with known digestive properties that grows wild in many gardens. Roman camomile (*Chamaemelum nobile*) is a perennial and is more common in Britain. It is a different species from German camomile but is used to treat similar conditions. German camomile is a useful plant to have to hand (it is much used in biodynamic gardening) and worth planting if you do not already have it. It can be sown from the end of winter onwards in a protected seedbed for later planting out or directly outside in spring. Alternatively, plants can be acquired from a nursery.

It is a robust plant that adapts to almost all soils and climates and does not need any special care, so long as the soil around it is kept damp and free of weeds. The flowers can be cut throughout spring and summer and spread on paper to dry in a cool and well-ventilated place. Once dry the flowers can be stored in hermetically sealing glass jars.

Caraway

Castor oil plant

Caraway belongs to the same family as anise and fennel and is outstanding for for its aromatic and anti-flatulence qualities. It is a hardy biennial and adapts to almost all soils, including poor ones, but grows best in a friable soil in a protected spot.

Its needs in terms of climate, manure, sowing and maintenance are similar to those described on page 67 for fennel and on page 88 for anise.

A castor oil bush can be included in a hedge of perennial medicinal plants (in cold zones it is grown as an annual). The seeds are highly toxic, however, so it is not recommended in school gardens or where children are likely to be.

It is easy to grow from seed in early spring and adapts to all soils, but prefers alkaline, well-drained ground and a sunny position. You need to keep an eye on its growth, as once installed it can be a somewhat invasive plant.

When the prickly sheaths open, the seeds can be collected and cut into pieces to lay next to green bean seeds as protection from weevils.

Comfrey

Coriander (cilantro)

Comfrey is also known as knitbone for its properties as a strengthener and knitter-together of bones. In the garden it is used as a mulch for tomato and potato plants because of its wealth of minerals, especially potassium. Comfrey tea, made by fermenting comfrey leaves in water and diluting the liquid with more water, is used as a revitalizing treatment for plants.

Comfrey is a vigorous perennial that in damp regions can become a weed that is difficult to eradicate. Plants need a lot of space as they can grow as high as 1.5m/5ft and can be 1–1.2m/39–48in wide. It grows well in cold climates but does not tolerate drought or excessive lime. The easiest way to grow it is by plant division in spring and autumn or by burying pieces of root which have one or more buds at the beginning of spring. Comfrey is a greedy plant and it is a good idea to give it regular feeds of compost (including immature compost). Its rapid growth from spring onwards means it is possible to make several cuttings of its large leaves.

Coriander is one of the easiest and most useful herbs to grow. Both leaves and seeds (crushed or whole) are widely used in Asian and South American cuisine. It is an important ingredient of curry and has anti-flatulence properties.

It is an annual that tolerates light frost and can grow up to 60cm/24in high. It grows well in loose, limey soils, protected from the wind. It will not survive being waterlogged and it dislikes nitrogen, so avoid sowing in recently manured beds. It benefits from potassium and needs plenty of sun.

Sow directly outside from March or April onwards; in hot zones it can be sown up until autumn. Sow in rows 30cm/12in apart, 1cm/½in or less deep; germination is slow. Thin to 12cm/5in between plants and keep weed free until the leaves cover the ground. You can start harvesting the leaves when plants are 20–30cm/8–12in high, before they begin to flower. Plants can be left to flower and form seeds to be harvested when plants dry out.

Echinacea

Elder

Echinacea is a wild plant from North America that has become popular in recent years for its antibiotic and disinfectant properties. It can be drunk as a juice or an infusion or made into decoctions and used to revitalize and protect garden plants. It is a perennial that grows from seed and once rooted reappears every year. Sow outside a few months before spring so that the cold prepares the seeds ready for germination. It adapts to almost all soils and climates and can tolerate extreme cold. It is worth putting in a prominent spot in the garden where its lovely red, orange and purple flowers can be enjoyed.

Elder is a bush worth planting in a hedge or some corner of the garden if there is none growing wild nearby. Its flowers, usually made into an infusion, have known anticatarrhal and sweat-producing properties, which put fevers to flight. The stems and leaves secrete enzymes which, once cut up and mixed with soil, help rooting, making a useful growing medium for cuttings. Mixing the cut-up leaves and stems with the soil in which potatoes are cultivated increases the potato harvest by as much as 40 per cent. It is easily propagated from softwood cuttings in early summer, semi-ripe cuttings in autumn or hardwood cuttings in winter. In March suckers growing at the base of an elder tree can also be dug up and planted. Cuttings/suckers need to be watered regularly until they have rooted well. It grows well in a sunny spot, but also grows in shade and resists cold and frost well. It prefers acidic, moist soils but can adapt to any soil. It has a tendency to produce a lot of bothersome branches; it is a good idea to cut away all but three or four central branches in the first few years. Later, all but one of these can be removed, leaving a single central trunk.

Hyssop

Hyssop is a hardy shrub and can be grown as part of a perennial hedge. It has expectorant properties and is used as an herb in the kitchen and also to spread biodynamic preparations (such as the hyssop used by priests for blessing). It can be grown from seed either in a unprotected seedbed or directly in the ground in early spring. It can also be grown from cuttings taken in spring. It likes warm climates and light, somewhat alkaline soils.

Lavender and lavendin

There are many different wild lavenders and also some natural hybrids known as lavendin that are differentiated by the size and vigour of the plants and the scent of the flowers. Two lavenders in particular are typical of the Mediterranean region. *Lavandula angustifolia* grows wild along the dry, stony hills bordering the Mediterranean, but is also happy in milder climates. *L. latifolia*, often called spike lavender, used to be the most popular medicinal species. Not fully hardy, it is rich in camphorated essential oils; the poorer the soil it grows in, the more concentrated the oils.

Lavenders prefer limestone soils, while lavendins are more tolerant of acidic and heavy soils. Both lavenders and lavendins do best in full sun and dislike intense cold or excessive humidity. They tend to live for five or six years and require little maintenance. In spring they can be pruned and fed some mature compost.

You can find plants in garden centres. They are easily propagated from cuttings. Take cuttings 12–15cm/5–6in long and 5mm in diameter from young branches of a mature plant (six to eight years old).

Cut flowers in the morning after the dew has dried and hang to dry in the shade. The dry flowers are used to make calming infusions, as an antiseptic and as an insect repellent – particularly to deter moths.

Lemon balm

Lemon verbena

Lemon balm is an exuberant perennial that gives off an intense lemon aroma when brushed against. Its flowers are very attractive to bees and its essence is used to repel mosquitoes and other insects (although contact with the plant can cause an allergic reaction in people with sensitive skin). Its principal use in herbal medicine is as a digestive (a very pleasant infusion can be made by combining it with mint, spearmint or lemon verbena).

Lemon balm adapts to all soils and climates and is extremely easy to propagate by plant division or from rhizomes, best done in autumn or in February. It also can be grown from seed sown in spring. If it has plenty of water and nutrients, it can become invasive like mint, so that it is better not planted in beds or between crops. Although a perennial, the plant does dry up in winter, so to have it available for infusions all year round cut some stalks just before flowering and hang up to dry.

This comes from America from the verbena family and grows as a bush. It loses its leaves in winter and shoots up again in spring. It likes hot and temperate climates and can easily grow 2–3m/7–10ft high. It needs a sunny spot, protected from the wind with plenty of space. It likes deep, humus-rich, loam soils. Every winter spread a centimetre or two of compost on the surface around the plant and cover it with a mulch of straw or other dry plants. It is easiest to grow from stem cuttings taken in August.

Marjoram

Mint

Marjoram is a very aromatic and tasty plant that often stands in for its first cousin oregano as a flavouring in pizzas, stews and salads. It is a hardy perennial that dies down in winter, shooting up again in spring. It grows well in almost any soil but prefers lime to acidic and does not need much in the way of compost. While it likes sun it also grows well in the shade. It is easy to grow from seed sown in spring, cuttings of non-flowering shoots taken in summer or by plant division in spring or autumn. Also stems in contact with the soil tend to develop roots and can be transplanted.

There are infinite varieties of mint and while almost all of them share the characteristic refreshing taste there are clear differences between the insipid water mint and the intensely flavoured peppermint or the aromatic and digestive spearmint.

All mints like deep, loamy, moist soils that are rich in humus. They grow well in full sun or semi-shade. They are easily grown from roots or by plant division or can be bought in garden centres. They are hardy perennial plants that tend to dry out in autumn/winter and sprout again in spring when they can be fed some compost. They are plants that, if given abundant water, will become invasive; some gardeners build brick walls around the plants some 30–40cm/12–16in deep and rising 30cm/12in above the level of the ground to stop roots spreading.

Nasturtium

Nettle

Nasturtium is a plant that is both ornamental and medicinal. It can be grown as ground cover or as a climber, and is a useful companion plant as it attracts aphids away from the crop and provides a habitat for ladybirds. Its vitamin-rich flowers have a peppery taste and can be eaten in salad. Nasturtium likes a sunny spot, although it also grows in the shade of fruit trees (which it protects from aphids). It does not like being flooded and does best in light, fertile, humus-rich soils. It is a half-hardy annual that can be easily grown from seed, cuttings or plant division. From early spring onwards it can be sown directly in place or in seedbeds for later planting out. It self-seeds easily.

There are many species of nettles. The perennial greater nettle or stinging nettle (*Urtica dioica*) is more typical of mountainous, rainy and rather cold regions and can grow as high as 1.2m/4ft, while the small, hardy annual dark-green dwarf nettle (*Urtica urens*) grows spontaneously in any soil rich in humus and decomposing organic matter. Nettles are rich in minerals, especially iron and calcium, and for centuries – until replaced by more succulent plants, such as spinach – they were an important part of the human diet.

Nettle tea, made by fermenting the leaves in water and diluting the liquid with more water, is much used as a tonic for plants and as a repellent for pests such as aphids. If nettles do not grow wild near by, it is worth cultivating a few stinging nettles in the medicinal garden in order to have it close at hand.

The easiest way to propagate nettle is by plant division. It is best to grow it in ground that has received plenty of leafmould or compost and has been covered with a mulch of organic matter, aiming for a lightly acidic soil.

Depending on local climate, nettles can be harvested two to four times a year, by cutting them 4–6cm/1–2m from the ground so that they sprout again strongly.

Rosemary

Sage

Mediterranean plant *par excellence*, rosemary should be planted in every garden. It has aromatic and medicinal properties, is hardy and easy to grow, and above all is attractive and generates a good presence.

Some herbalists call rosemary the European ginseng, for its stimulating action on physical and mental vitality. Its use as a culinary herb is well known and rosemary tincture (made with camphorated alcohol) is ideal for rubbing on bruises and sore backs and as a relaxant for muscular tension. One of the best reasons for having a few plants of rosemary around the garden or in pots on the balcony is that the beautiful intense blue flowers attract pollinating insects that go on to pollinate your tomatoes and courgette plants, helping to increase the garden´s fertility and productivity.

Rosemary is a perennial shrub that likes a sunny spot and grows in any soil, but with a preference for the dry and stony. It does less well in moist, heavy soils: even here, provided drainage is good, the plant can grow exuberantly, but the active and aromatic properties are less concentrated than when it is grown in poor, dry soils. Rosemary can be grown from seed, but the most common way is from cuttings (it roots relatively easily). It can also be easily found in garden centres.

It needs little care or water. You need only cut out the odd old branch and mulch the bush with pine bark or, better still, pine needles.

Sage has seemingly endless therapeutic properties. It can be used as an antiseptic, for healing scars, as a tonic, as an astringent or for its wealth of antioxidants. There are many varieties of sage and you can make flowering clumps using four or five types of differing size, colour and smell. It grows well in hot and temperate climates and tolerates drought and mild frosts. It is generally undemanding but does not like damp or very poorly drained soil. It is easy to grow from seed sown in February or March in a seedbed and pricked out and transplanted to open ground or into pots. It can also be grown from cuttings taken at the beginning of spring or by plant division at the end of winter. However, the easiest method is simply to cut and transplant branches that have spontaneously rooted where they touch the ground.

It is interesting to grow sage next to rosemary and thyme, as they mutually boost each other´s growth. You need to take care where you plant sage, as it develops into a big bush and its roots generate chemical substances that inhibit the growth of some crops (and other aromatic plants and trees). It should not be grown in beds or between crops. From time to time it can be given a good pruning.

Stevia

Stevia, a member of the chrysanthemum family, comes originally from South America. *Stevia rebaudiana* 'Bertoni', called in Guarani *ka'a he'e* (meaning 'sweet herb'), is one of more than three hundred varieties to be found in the forest straddling Paraguay and Brazil. Its characteristic sweet taste (it is fifteen times sweeter than sugar used fresh, and fifty times sweeter when dried) comes from the active ingredients in the leaves, which the Guarani Indians use for sweetening and also give to their children to suck.

Stevia appears to lower blood sugar levels and hypertension, and has antiseptic, diuretic, anti-inflammatory and antioxidant properties. Studies in Japan suggest it increases soil fertility, cleans contaminated ground and increases resistance to pests.

Stevia seeds have poor germination rates but the plant can be easily cultivated from cuttings. In summer take cuttings 10cm/4in long from stems that have not yet flowered, trim off the leaves and stick the cuttings in pots of potting compost. Keep in a warm shaded place, watering the pots regularly but avoiding excessive humidity until the cuttings take root. Stevia needs similar growing conditions to basil (page 88) and will grow back in spring for four or five years. Although it is a subtropical plant it adapts well to the Mediterranean climate. Autumn is the best time for harvesting and drying the leaves. Spraying garden plants with diluted macerations and decoctions of stevia has an invigorating effect.

Tansy

Tansy is a variety of chrysanthemum found growing wild in parts of the Mediterranean. Its flower heads contain natural pyrethrins, which make it useful as a natural insecticide. Its presence repels pests from garden plants and stimulates flowering in roses and strawberries. It can be planted in the medicinal garden or next to ornamental plants (it produces a stunning display of yellow flowers against a mass of green foliage). Its flowers can be made into a decoction to spray on plants attacked by aphids and other pests. The flowers can also be picked and dried in the shade to use as needed or crushed up and sprinkled on seeds kept for sowing. It is a hardy perennial and grows well in most types of soil and adapts to most climates (it can be invasive). It can be grown from seed sown in spring, from cuttings or by plant division in autumn.

Thyme

Valerian

Since time immemorial thyme's therapeutic qualities have been known and made use of. It is one of the most powerful antiseptics and anti-catarrhals that nature offers us. It grows wild in much of the Mediterranean and is easily harvested and dried. It can also be grown in a sunny spot in the medicinal garden in order to have it to hand. The small hardy varieties have more medicinal properties than the more exuberant cultivated ones. Thyme is a perennial that grows well in almost all soils and needs little care. It is easy to grow from seed or plant division in spring or from cuttings in early summer.

Valerian provides the most popular natural remedy for stress and nervous tension. It is a hardy perennial that can easily grow 1m/39in tall and has either white or violet flowers.

It likes deep, cool, humus-rich soils and is relatively easy to grow. Provide plants with plenty of compost and water regularly. It can be grown in a clump by itself or along with other large medicinal plants such as tansy, rosemary or lavender. It can be propagated by plant division or from runners in autumn, but the easiest method is to let it self-seed, which it does with enthusiasm.

Winter savory

Wormwood and mugwort

Winter savory is an aromatic perennial herb native to the Mediterranean. It is a robust. hardy plant that grows well in all types of soil but does best in a lime soil with good exposure to sun. It can be propagated from seed (sown under glass in late winter or early spring) or from cuttings or by plant division in spring and autumn. It is also easy to find in plant nurseries. Savory is traditionally used in the Mediterranean to flavour olives but it is also good with meats and in salads and bean dishes, and it has useful digestive, antiseptic and tonic properties. It can be used fermented or in decoctions as a stimulant. However, it should be avoided in pregnancy.

Wormwood and mugwort are related perennial plants and both are notably bitter. They are hardy, drying up in winter to sprout again in spring. They have been much used against pests, especially for the control of aphids and to deter cabbage white butterflies and codling moth from laying eggs.

Wormwood grows best and has more active properties when grown in dry conditions, while mugwort, like most garden plants, prefers a watered, manured soil. They can be grown from seed in a protected seedbed at the end of winter and pricked out into containers when 6–10cm/2½–4in tall for planting out when they have developed good root formation. They can also be grown by plant division in late winter/early spring. When the plant is at least 40cm/16in tall it can be harvested by cutting stems of leaves and flowers from the middle of summer onwards. It can be used immediately or dried for later use. It is best not to put leaves or branches of wormwood or mugwort on the compost heap, or to grow them near the compost heap, as they contain substances that inhibit fermentation.

THE ORCHARD

GROWING FRUIT TREES

A book such as this is not able to go into the same detail as a treatise devoted to organic fruit growing. However, for those who have enough space for a small orchard it can give some guidelines and the key points to bear in mind in order to benefit from fresh fruit for most of the year.

In a very small garden, it does not make much sense to plant trees. The shade cast by the trees and the avid take-up of nutrients by the roots would make it difficult, and eventually impossible, to grow vegetables.

If you have a little more space it is well worth thinking about planting some fruit trees, especially along the northern edge of the garden, where the shade cast will not be a serious problem. It is still advisable to make your selection from small trees such as plum, pear,

orange or mandarin. Avoid trees such as fig, walnut and cherry, which if uncontrolled can get very large. Vines or espalier trees (pruned to grow in one plane) can be grown along walls or fences, taking up little space.

Planning the orchard

Aesthetically pleasing though it might be to contemplate an apple tree in blossom in the middle of the garden, such a tree is not a practical proposition in a vegetable garden. A better option is to plant trees on the edges of the garden or, better still, to create an orchard with a variety of trees or different types of the same species. In a family garden the aim is to have a selection of fresh and healthy fruit throughout the year. In a small orchard you could plant, for example, a cherry tree and one or two apricots – these will bear fruit in May and June; a nectarine – June and July; two peach trees – June to

September; two apple trees – August and September; a clementine and a mandarin – September and October; an orange tree – October to March; a lemon tree – all year; a persimmon – September to November; and a fig tree – August and September. Between the larger trees or around the edge you can plant dwarf trees, or soft fruit bushes such as raspberries.

Problems with fruit trees

While plagues of pests are rare among vegetables, the same cannot be said about fruit trees. Most fruit tree varieties are the result of continuous selection and forcing by means of constant pruning. The result is big, sweet, juicy fruit, far removed from the small, bitter, hard fruit of their wild ancestors. The modern fruit tree is a much-debilitated life form, heavily dependent on the farmer's or gardener's care. The disappearance of native, rustic varieties adapted to local conditions and their replacement by standardized varieties as well as a generally deteriorating environment have only aggravated the situation.

In commercial fruit production an apple can receive between fifteen and thirty different phytosanitary treatments (insecticides, fungicides, etc.). These are while it is still growing on the tree; afterwards it is submerged in chemical solutions to ensure its preservation in refrigerated containers until the moment of distribution. In addition to these there are the treatments the tree receives in winter and at flowering. Big plantations and regions devoted to fruit growing, with hundreds of kilometres of orange, apple or pear monocultures, have had an effect on the specialization of pathogens, making control very difficult. In addition, where pesticide use has been excessive pests have developed resistance to them.

Yet another problem is the international trade in exotic fruit. This has resulted in a transfer of pest plagues to places where they were unknown and where there is no natural regulating mechanism. The citrus leaf miner is a clear example of this.

The truth is that it is not easy to produce healthy fruit without fighting against a series of enemies, some of which can be devastating. Against some enemies, such as aphids or birds, there are more or less effective

Fruit tree pests

Local varieties of fruit trees cultivated organically should not present too many problems. However, recently, plagues of Mediterranean fruit fly and similar pests have caused worm infestation of all types of fruit. In addition to the normal preventative practices of organic agriculture (see page 50), an effective measure is to bag the fruit while still green and hang up fly traps containing some food stuff.

means at our disposal. However, there are other pests that are very damaging, such as the Mediterranean fruit fly. From the beginning of the hot season these lay eggs in all sweet mature fruit they encounter and prevent the development of apricots, plums, figs, peaches, nectarines and even oranges. The codling moth causes the same problems as the medfly but in apple and pear trees. Food or pheromone traps are expensive and are often not enough to combat the plague; pheromone traps have also been found to be effective only when used in large areas of fruit trees. Seeing trees laden with fruit only to find, on biting into a mature fruit, that it has a 'lodger' can be quite disheartening. In a small orchard good results can be obtained by covering the trees with mosquito nets or covering individual fruit with paper bags, though some of the orchard's charm is inevitably lost.

Problem-free fruit trees

Fruit trees for a family garden rather than commercial exploitation can be grouped into those that give more problems and those that are relatively problem-free. The most delicate and problematic include peach, apple and pear. The least demanding include fig, cherry, persimmon and apricot (except for the late-maturing varieties, which are susceptible to fruit fly attack). The avocado is also fairly problem-free but requires relatively high average temperatures and is susceptible to intense cold and hard frosts. The kiwi, contrary to what one would imagine, needs a humid climate and a shady spot but otherwise presents no particular problem.

Apples do best when subjected to frost in winter.

Choosing fruit trees

Choosing which fruit trees to plant is no easy task. The choice available in nurseries is very limited; there may be only some three or four varieties of pear and five or six of apple or peach. This is despite the fact that there are thousands of varieties of apples, pears and peaches and hundreds of types of oranges and clementines. Sadly the standardization of production and consumers´ tastes has meant that the majority of native varieties are disappearing in the drive for greater productivity, profits and ease of distribution.

For fruit trees, as for vegetables, it is important to know the climatic conditions, the kind of soil and the microclimate of your garden. This enables you to choose which varieties of fruit trees are most suitable and which rootstocks to use for grafting. As far as possible choose the least exotic varieties. You will be much safer with trees that are already adapted to the local climate and with rootstocks that tolerate the acidity or alkalinity of the soil well and are resistant to the most common problems, such as drought or excessive humidity.

Plant or sow?

There are numerous advantages to sowing the future rootstock and grafting on to it yourself (see page 108). Most importantly you can choose the most appropriate variety for the rootstock and by sowing it *in situ* you can avoid the risk of damaging the roots through transplanting. The tree´s roots will be deeper than those of transplanted trees, which tend to have a more horizontal root development. However, all this does demand patience, as instead of having fruit in two or three years you must wait five or six. To quote Elton Trueblood, 'A man has made at least a start on discovering the meaning of human life when he plants shade trees under which he knows full well he will never sit.'

If you opt for buying grafted trees ready for planting here are some guidelines to follow.

- Avoid big, exuberant trees, especially those that already have fruit.
- Choose robust-looking trees, either in pots or bare- rooted.
- Bare-root trees are cheaper and their roots are more extended; however, they can only be planted when the tree is dormant.
- Avoid trees with bark damage or spindly branches.
- If the tree is to go in a place with good soil in or close to the garden where it will receive plenty of care and watering, then it is possible to choose an exuberant tree that has been somewhat forced in the nursery with fertilizer and watering. If the tree is destined for some more distant location, where it will not receive abundant watering or where the soil is poor, it is better to choose a hardier, less exuberant specimen.
- The younger the tree is at the time of transplanting, the greater its chances are of rooting well.
- Trees that have been grafted for a year tend to give the best results and soon overtake older trees transplanted from pots. Look carefully at where the tree has been grafted to make sure that the wound has healed properly and there are no cracks or strange bumps.

Planting a tree

1 Dig a hole two or three times the size of the tree´s root system. The hole should be at least 40 x 40 x 40cm/16 x 16 x 16in, or better still 60 x 60 x 60cm/24 x 24 x 24in. Make separate piles of topsoil and subsoil, and be methodical, for instance always putting topsoil to the right and subsoil to the left. The depth of the hole is also dependent on the type of soil. In dry, arid zones it should be deeper and in humid zones shallower. In humid regions the tree can be planted in a little mound to avoid root asphyxiation.

2 In dry, loose soils it is a good idea to put a layer of leafmould or well-broken-down compost at the bottom of the hole. This acts like a sponge and helps retain moisture. In moist, compacted soils put a layer of gravel or pebbles at the bottom of the hole to help drainage and avoid root asphyxiation.

3 Mix some leafmould with the pile of dug-out subsoil and deposit some of this mixture on top of the compost or gravel.

4 Place the tree in the hole with its roots sitting on the soil, making sure that it is vertical. Put a stick across the hole to check that the tree is at the right depth – the soil should come to the same point on the trunk as it did in the nursery.

5 Prune back any damaged roots.

6 For the next step either enlist the help of someone to support the tree or make a makeshift support in the form of a pyramid with bamboo or whatever comes to hand. Backfill the hole with the rest of the soil mix. The graft must be a few centimetres above ground level. In humid areas where the tree is planted on a mound, or in windy places where the trunk is supported around the base, the extra height needs to be taken into account. Otherwise the tree will put out roots above the graft and cancel the function of the rootstock, which will eventually rot.

7 Finish filling the hole with the topsoil, to which has been added a third of well-broken-down compost. Tread the soil down firmly and water immediately.

8 In dry areas it is advisable to make a small depression around the tree to act as a reservoir for when it is watered and for any sporadic rainfall. After a few years when the tree has become established, the depression can be filled in with soil mixed with

Growing trees and bushes

- To reduce maintenance work, avoid planting invasive trees and bushes.
- Transplant bare-root trees and bushes in autumn or spring, but never when they are in an active growing stage.
- Before transplanting, water the plant so that the soil sticks to the roots. Bind the branches as tightly as possible without causing damage.

compost, leaving it level. In humid, rainy areas the mound can be finished with additional soil mixed with some sand – if the soil is very compacted – and some mature compost.

9 In very windy areas or areas subject to storms it is advisable to stake the tree. Use string or straps, being careful not to tie them too tightly in order not to damage the bark.

10 Finish the operation by laying down a mulch of withered or dry organic matter – grass cuttings, straw, pine needles or comfrey leaves (however, see problems with mulching below).

Care with digging

Digging in the proximity of fruit trees can cause serious problems, as it damages the superficial roots of the tree, producing wounds through which disease can easily enter. One option is to leave an area around the trunk covered with a permanent mulch and strim the rest of the orchard (or leave ducks and hens to roam there).

Pros and cons of mulching fruit trees

Mulching helps transplanted trees stay free of competing weeds. By providing shade it also keeps the soil cooler, thus reducing the amount of watering necessary. However, it can present a problem in very dry areas where the tree is dependent on sporadic rainfall. The organic matter acts like a sponge and does not allow the scarce amount of rain to penetrate through the mulch to the ground. As soon as the sun comes up the dry air rapidly dehydrates the mulch and the tree can end up suffering endemic thirst. In such a situation a better solution is a mulch of stones. Failing that the tree will need watering from time to time. Watering into a large water container placed upside down with the neck buried in the earth is a good way to ensure that a young tree gets the moisture it needs.

Other means of propagation

Propagation of fruit trees by means of seeds results in considerable genetic variation and a tendency to revert to the wild form. There is also the problem of seedless fruit. In order to reproduce fruit trees, you need to use techniques that will result in fruit with the desired characteristics such as taste, hardiness or resistance to pests.

There are various methods of propagation, such as layering, as described on page 41. Another method is to cut from the tree a one- or two-year-old branch that is well developed and already has buds. Partly bury it and in a short time it should develop roots. Other types of cuttings are also possible. Compound layering (bending the stem into the soil as for simple layering but alternately covering and exposing sections of the stem) is suitable for plants with long, flexible shoots, such as vines.

However, many of these methods produce plants that are less vigorous and robust, or are more susceptible to pathogens. For this reason the normal practice is to use plants propagated by these methods as rootstocks, later grafting on to them. An alternative and preferable, though slower, method is to sow seeds of wild or resistant plants and when they have reached a certain stage of development graft the desired cultivar on to them.

Grafting

Grafting is perhaps the simplest method of reproducing a fruit variety so that it maintains most of its qualities. It consists of inserting a segment of a plant which has one or more buds into a rootstock of a compatible species. In grafting, the cambium layers of the two different segments are aligned and grow together, forming one plant. Natural grafting occurs where two branches are in close contact over several years.

Advantages of grafting:

- It can produce more vigorous, pest-resistant and earlier fruiting trees.
- Old trees can be rejuvenated by means of grafting.
- By grafting a branch of a different variety or one that produces male flowers on to a female tree you can ensure pollination of trees that are not self-fertile.
- It can be used to establish, extend or multiply interesting varieties or ones that are sterile (i.e. do not produce seeds).
- Using suitable rootstocks, you can grow trees

Approach grafting   Whip-and-tongue grafting   Splice grafting   Shield budding

Crown grafting   Patch budding   Side grafting

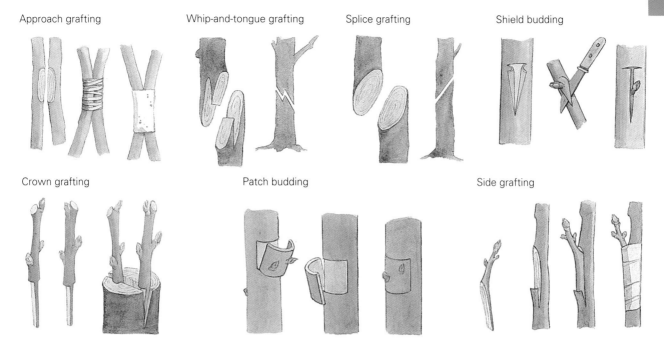

even in poor soils and in difficult conditions such as drought.

- The size of the tree can be controlled by the choice of rootstock.
- Grafting can improve the cultivar; for example, a mandarin grafted on to a lemon produces earlier, bigger and sweeter fruit.
- Plants that have trouble rooting (from cuttings, for example) can be propagated by grafting.
- Different varieties of fruit can be grown on the same tree – for example, skilled grafting can give you a fig tree that produces white, black, purple and green figs or an orange tree that has a branch of navel oranges and another of navelate oranges. (It is worth noting, however, that such trees tend to be weaker.)

Grafting in practice Grafting, although a technical task requiring knowledge and experience, also has an aura of magic and sensitivity about it.

Grafting should not be done when the plant is fully active or when fully dormant; spring and autumn are the best times. Choose a day that is neither too hot nor too damp.

It is important that the part to be grafted (or scion wood) is compatible with the rootstock. For example,

loquat and quince are compatible, as are hawthorn and pear or almond and peach. Apple and peach are not; nor are holm oak and plum.

Also, different grafting methods work better for different types of tree.

Whatever type of graft used (refer to a specialist book if necessary), the cambium layers of the two plants must be in contact (cambium is the layer of tissue just below the bark and is where the tree grows). Scar tissue develops at the point of contact, forming a close bond.

To ensure that the scion wood stays in place and to stop the cut ends from drying out, tie damp raffia around the join. Cover the whole joint, including buds, with a special grafting paste containing wax and propolis or a mixture of clay and cow dung. When the graft is established and the bud has sprouted, remove the raffia, taking care, as the union will still be fragile. Remove any roots that have grown from the join and any unwanted buds from the graft. These are all simple tasks but ones that require experience and green fingers.

It is worth experimenting with grafting even if just for the pleasure of doing it. It is also a way of preserving cultivars that are in danger of dying out through not being of commercial interest.

Pruning

Whether or not to prune is a matter of controversy, but pruning does offer a number of advantages. By making trees a manageable size it makes them easier to work with; it lets in light and ventilation; and it avoids excessive growth of leaves and branches to the detriment of fruit production. Some followers of permaculture and natural farming methods disagree with conventional pruning methods, considering them unnatural. Instead, they advocate leaving a tree to develop freely. There is something to be said for this argument, but it can mean having no room to grow anything else, as the shade cast by a tree can take up a lot of space. If you have several hectares at your disposal, you can leave trees to grow freely, especially cherry, apricot, fig, walnut and plum trees. However, if you have only a small plot, there is no choice but to resort to rootstocks that limit the tree's growth and pruning to limit the space it occupies and make the tree as productive as possible.

In fact most fruit trees that are not pruned will give fruit only on alternate years. Between the two extremes (no human interference and abusive or devitalizing pruning) there is a middle way. This is to carry out a limited pruning regularly that orientates the tree to grow in a coherent form in harmony with its setting and, as far as possible, encourages the production of healthy, tasty and abundant fruit.

Moderate pruning encourages fruit production.

It is worth bearing in mind that pruning, or the removal of branches, shoots and buds, is a normal occurrence in nature, where it is caused by storms, strong winds or certain animals that feed off parts of the trees. What is perhaps further removed from nature is heavy winter pruning, where the cutting of thick branches inflicts on the tree serious wounds that subsequently have great trouble healing. On the other hand, light summer pruning of terminal leaf buds and branches and shoots no longer than 30–40cm/12–16in would seem reasonable. In branches longer than 60cm/24in the sap is unable to change direction, so that when such branches are removed water shoots appear, caused by the excess of sap.

It should be remembered that trees – and indeed most plants – have properties which mean that the trunk, branches and leaves all act as antennae that pick up cosmic and atmospheric energies and radiations. At the same time the roots act as an 'earth', taking up the electric energy and radiations coming from the subsoil. Thus when we destroy the natural disposition of a tree in a brusque fashion serious energy imbalances are created, affecting the sap and at a more subtle level the tree or plant's ability to relate harmoniously with its environment.

Pruning for form and for fruit production

Pruning is initially aimed at the tree's correct formation and development and later towards maximizing fruit production. Formative pruning or training helps make the tree sturdier, making good yields possible without exhausting the tree. It also creates airy spaces within the tree, letting sunlight reach in to the mass of leaves and fruit. In general it is best to opt for keeping the trees low enough to make intervention and harvesting easier.

In the first three or four years it is best to get rid of flowers and fruit in the first stage of their development, giving priority to developing a strong structure at the cost of having a harvest. Hard though this might seem, in the long term you will benefit from a stronger, healthier, more fertile tree.

Pruning tips

- When pruning a big branch, first cut off bits of it to lessen the weight. Then make a cut on the underside of the branch so that the bark is not torn away when the upper cut is made.
- When cutting out big branches, leave a nearby twig to draw up the sap.
- On old plants go round the edges of a cut with a knife and anoint with a paste of propolis and clay. The cut will heal better.
- Pruning and pinching out weak bushes in a waning moon makes them grow stronger.
- Weak parts benefit from strong pruning to stimulate growth, while mature growth needs only light pruning.
- To renovate a hedge, hard prune on one side one year and on the other the next.

Pruning for fruit production, or maintenance pruning, is done when the principal branches are well formed. Doing it before induces premature ageing in the tree. Successive pruning for fruit production guarantees regular harvests, avoiding excessive harvests one year and then nothing for two years. The pruning stimulates new vegetative growth to replace older wood whose fruit production is decreasing. It needs to be done in an intelligent way that respects the overall structure and does not weaken the tree. Often simply bending the branches is enough to stimulate fruit production without having to resort to pruning. Vertical branches suck up sap and tend not to produce fruit.

There are many possibilities and variations when it comes to pruning, both for form and for fruit production. For specialized technical help, you must look beyond this book (turning to specialist volumes such as *The Backyard Orchardist* by Stella Otto). It is also worth acknowledging that it is sometimes very difficult to relate drawings of how to prune trees to the actual tree in front of you. A friend with some experience to guide you through the first steps is invaluable.

Apple

Apples (*Malus sylvestris*) have numerous nutritional and therapeutic properties but only when grown organically. Commercial apple growing in the Mediterranean involves the use and abuse of chemical fertilizers and pesticides to an extent that is frankly frightening, as described on page 105.

Apple trees need a period of winter dormancy and heavy frosts to enable the trees to produce healthy, vigorous spring shoots and also to control pest populations. When apples are cultivated in the hot or temperate Mediterranean climate, the trees are almost bound to be weak and need endless care in order to survive. However, you might well still want to try growing apple trees, if only for the pleasure of seeing apple blossom in spring. And there are a few well-adapted though usually non-commercial varieties like the 'Cirri' that grow well in temperate climates and barely suffer from pests. Note that if you are hoping for fruit as well as blossom, to ensure pollination you will need to plant at least two trees of different varieties, as apples are not self-fertile.

Climate As mentioned, apples prefer cold climates and tolerate winter temperatures as low as –20˚C/-4˚F. They need a period of winter dormancy, which is not possible in warm coastal areas.

Soil Apple trees like cool, fertile, deep and permeable soils. They do not flourish in heavy or very compacted soils or in soils that are too loose and sandy. Nor do they like shallow or excessively alkaline soils. Poor soils can, of course, be improved by the addition of compost and organic matter. Grafting certain varieties on to specific rootstocks is another way to adapt apple trees to a less than ideal soil.

Watering Apart from the watering necessary at the first stages after sowing or planting, apple trees should not need watering if grown in favourable climates where there is frequent rain. If cultivating apples in dry regions or in fast-draining stony terrain, it is a good idea to install a drip irrigation system and maintain a permanent mulch.

Propagation Propagation by seed results in wild apple trees and sometimes a new and interesting variety that can be multiplied by means of grafting. Trees grown from seed do not give fruit until six or seven years after sowing, which rather limits this method to tree nurseries.

Among the classic rootstocks there are three that are most commonly used. These are the seedling rootstock (grafted with shoots of resistant, vigorous varieties), which makes possible large trees that adapt very well to deep soils; 'Doucin', which is used to obtain medium-sized trees and allows trees to be grown on either acidic or alkaline soils; and 'Paradise', which is used to grow dwarf varieties and needs a cool, fertile soil. 'Doucin' can also be used for dwarf forms in dry terrains. Trees grafted on to this variety tend to fruit in the third or fourth year, while those grafted on to 'Paradise' rootstock fruit in the second or third year after being grafted. However, the 'Doucin' rootstock gives trees that live longer. Quince, hawthorn and pear rootstocks are also possible choices, but they are usually not as successful as those mentioned above.

Grafting is normally done by shield budding in August. It can also be done by crown grafting and by using wedge-shaped scions.

Planting Ideally sow seeds or plant shoots of healthy, resistant trees directly where they are to grow and later graft the desired varieties on to them.

If buying already grafted trees from a nursery, make sure they have a good soil root ball. Moving a tree with no soil around the roots is very stressful for the tree and can weaken it for life.

It is best to dig planting holes months in advance. Large trees are usually planted 5m/16ft apart, medium-sized trees 3m/10ft apart and dwarf or bush varieties every 1.5–2m/5–7ft. Dwarf and bush varieties can be grown in the middle of deep beds with vegetables on either side.

Pruning Formation pruning is very similar to that for pear trees (page 130). In big plantations the central leader (trunk) is cut back to 80–150cm/32in–5ft; a horizontal cordon is the most suitable method for supported trees.

Instead of pruning for fruit production it is less traumatic for the tree if you bend the branches, making them more horizontal. Pinch off terminal buds so that regrowth is from the upper buds and the young shoots. The tree should produce fruiting buds the second year. After fruiting these can be cut back to three buds so that new fruiting branches are formed.

Care and maintenance It is a good idea to maintain a permanent mulch around the trunks of apple and most other trees during the first three years. Dig or weed around the tree (never less than 1m/39in from the trunk) to keep the soil cool and free from competing weeds. You can also sow a green manure in autumn or winter beyond the mulched part to be incorporated into the soil in spring.

From the fifth year, or whenever the trees are well developed, a permanent green cover using a leguminous plant such as white clover is a good plan. In the first years it is possible to grow vegetables in the free spaces between the outer reaches of the trees' canopies (although some gardeners would not recommend doing this). When the trees get bigger this practice must be abandoned, as digging can damage trees' roots; the vegetables also suffer, as the trees take up most of the available nutrients and the shade cast reduces the light available.

Harvesting and storage Apples are usually harvested as they begin to ripen. Early varieties can be harvested in July/August and late varieties in September/October. Pick fruit manually, if possible retaining the stalk with the apple (it keeps better) and taking care not to damage the branches.

If you have only a couple of apple trees the fruit can be stored in boxes with straw (a single layer per box). Keep the boxes in a cool, dark place and store only undamaged apples, with their stalks. The ideal temperature for storage is 4°C/39°F, but the only inconvenience caused by higher temperatures is that the apples ripen faster. Overripe and split apples can be stewed and frozen or put in sterilized jars.

Problems Apple trees grown using organic gardening methods in favourable soil and climatic conditions should not be problematic. Both pests and diseases are minimal compared to those that attack conventional monocultures.

Apples are similar to pears in how they are affected by adverse climatic conditions and diseases such as rust and scab. As regards pests, apples are prey to apple worms and to codling moths, which lay their eggs around young shoots or flowers and end up attacking the fruit. Sowing wild asparagus below apple trees keeps codling moth at bay. Strips of corrugated cardboard tied around the trunks and main branches at the end of summer provide a refuge for caterpillars that can be removed and burnt in the middle or end of the autumn. Preventative treatments of Bordeaux mixture can also be applied.

Green aphids may attack young shoots in May. Make sure trees are not overwatered or receiving too much nitrogen. In severe cases apply a natural insecticide. The woolly apple aphid, coated in a white spongy down, is one of the most problematic. The eggs overwinter in cracks under the bark of the tree and the larvae appear in spring. The larvae can multiply very rapidly and in a short time completely invade the tree. The tree ends up covered in protuberances and might not survive. It is necessary to intervene promptly to avoid serious damage and although it is difficult to get rid of the pest completely, natural insecticides are useful. The ideal solution would be to encourage the pest's natural predator, the insect *Aphelinus mali*, and carry out preventative actions such as brushing down the trunk and main branches and covering them with a paste made of clay, lime and powdered lithothamne, a marine carbonate. This paste is effective against pests and also invigorates the tree.

Apricot

The apricot (*Prunus armeniaca*) is a deciduous tree that can often be seen growing in abandoned smallholdings. Although the delicious, sweet fruit matures and needs to be harvested over a short period, it can be preserved by drying for use throughout the year.

The apricot is a tree that is very well adapted to the Mediterranean climate. When left to grow freely it can reach a height of over 8m/26ft, although in poor soil it stays smaller. It is usually self-pollinating and can be grown with other trees or by itself in a sunny spot.

Climate It needs a temperate or hot climate and as it flowers early it does not tolerate late frosts. For the same reason too much ambient humidity is not desirable.

Soil It likes a light, warm, fertile soil that drains well. Lime-clay soils or lime-stony soils suit it well. It is not productive in heavy, cold, damp and poorly draining soils.

Watering It does not usually require watering and too much moisture is harmful.

Propagation Trees grown from seed can produce tasty fruits but often they are too acidic, so using rootstocks is recommended. Wild apricot seeds can be sown directly in place to provide rootstocks in light, dry soils. In deep, lime soils sow seeds of wild almond and in damp soils sow seeds of plum. Later the desired variety can be grafted on to the rootstock, using shield budding, preferably in August.

Planting If you opt for trees from a nursery, choose trees that are two or three years old and plant 4–8m/13–26ft apart, depending on variety.

Pruning Apricots are trees that grow stupendously with barely any human intervention. Old dry branches or those that are in the way can be cut out, but avoid big cuts, which can provoke gumming.

Care and maintenance Apricots do not need or appreciate digging around the trunks. A permanent vegetal mulch for the first few years stops weeds growing and keeps the soil loose, cool and fed.

Harvesting Depending on variety and climatic region, apricots are mature and ready to be harvested from May until July. For drying, the fruit is best picked when not entirely ripe (a solar dryer works very well – see page 143). The fruit on trees that are not watered starts to dry on the tree or on falling to the ground. It is always a good idea to scald the fruit with boiling water before drying it, to get rid of parasites and make it less likely to spoil.

Problems Apricot trees are, on the whole, unproblematic. Most worrying, perhaps, is the gum the tree sometimes produces as a result of bad pruning or simply from being pruned. In humid areas the tree can suffer from silver leaf, a fungal disease that produces white marks on the leaves and fruit. Silver leaf can be controlled by applying Bordeaux mixture and collecting and burning the affected leaves and fruit. Pests include woodworm and moth, similar to those of pear trees. Most problematic is the Mediterranean fruit fly. This appears with the arrival of hot weather and lays its eggs in ripening fruit. The fruit fills with larvae and soon rots, and entire harvests can be lost. The best prevention is to choose early varieties of apricot that are harvested in May, as from June onwards the fruit fly can be an unstoppable plague. You can also try minimizing the problem by hanging on the south side of the tree yellow traps soaked in sugar and natural insecticides or some sticky substance.

Avocado

The avocado (*Persea americana*), besides having many vitamins, has a high proportion of proteins and fats, which is uncommon in fresh fruit. It (or some of its many varieties) can be cultivated anywhere oranges fruit successfully. It is a curious thing that most gardeners in the Mediterranean will grow apple trees in their orchard knowing how problematic they are but it will not even occur to them to try cultivating an avocado tree or two, despite the fact that they are hardly any trouble and provide good yields.

There are many types of avocado, distinguishable by the form or size of the fruit, the texture of the skin (smooth or wrinkled), the country of origin (Guatemala, Mexico, West Indies), and its resistance to cold, soil alkalinity or acidity, etc. The choice available makes it easier to find one or more varieties that are suitable for the climate and soil of your garden.

The commonest problem you might encounter if you plant only one avocado tree in your orchard is that some trees are not self-pollinating and need a tree with male flowers in the vicinity. It is difficult to know if your tree is self-pollinating or not, unless you buy it from a tree nursery with a guarantee. However, with the first flowering it will become apparent, and if it is not self-pollinating there is always the solution of grafting on to it the branch of a male flowering tree.

Other advantages of growing avocado trees are their great productivity and early harvest. The harvest is staggered from October until March, a time when other fresh, dense fruit is scarce.

Climate Avocados love above all sun and heat, and fear cold, frost and strong winds. While they grow where orange trees flourish, their branches and leaves are more fragile and less robust than those of oranges. They need to be protected from the cold from the north and from strong winds by means of hedges, windbreaks, etc. Their resistance to cold depends on the variety; Mexican avocados are the most resistant (they can tolerate between –3° and –7°C/26° and 19°F) and West Indian are the most delicate and suffer damage when temperatures drop below –1° or –2°/30° or 28°F.

Soil Avocadoes do better in acidic soils with a pH between 6 and 7. In alkaline soils they tend to suffer from chlorosis and from iron and zinc deficiency. If possible, find a site with medium-textured, deep soil that is neither loose nor compacted. Heavy, ill-draining soils are not recommended, as flooding of the roots can be very damaging and can cause them to rot. Nor are sandy or saline soils recommended.

Manure/compost Given the size the trees reach and their productivity, it is important not to neglect the fertility of the soil where they grow. In autumn and spring spread 1–3kg/2¼–7lb of compost per 1m²/11ft² on the ground around the trunk as far as the tree canopy reaches. Given how delicate and superficial the roots are, it is best to cover the compost with a mulch and leave earthworms to incorporate the compost into the soil rather than digging it in.

Watering Avocado trees need regular watering because of their great foliar mass and the high rate of water loss from the leaves. However, avoid flooding the trees; drip irrigation is perhaps the best method.

Propagation If you are considering sowing the stone of a shop-bought avocado, be warned: it is very

115

likely that the tree will not live more than a few years, as the rootstock will not be very resistant. If the tree is still alive four or five years on, it might surprise you with a new variety of fruit that is exceptional, or inedible. In addition the tree will produce fruit only in alternate years. In tree nurseries seeds of resistant varieties are normally used, such as 'Topa-Topa', 'Mexicola' (the most resistant to cold and fungal diseases), 'Lula' (tolerates saline and lime soils better) and, in Spain, a local variety.

Planting Trees in pots can be transplanted at any time except during the coldest months. The best months are March and April. It should be remembered that the tree canopy can easily reach 10–12m/33–40ft in diameter, which can be a problem in a small orchard.

Grafting Grafting can be by shield budding, crown or lateral graft; the most classic way, which gives best results, is by wedge (cleft) graft. The best month for grafting is March.

Pruning Avocado trees develop a good structure and do not need pruning. Branches grow in a tortuous, sinuous fashion, but this need not concern you. You need only to cut out the odd badly situated branch at the beginning of the tree's formation.

Care and maintenance Except for its susceptibility to intense cold and strong winds the avocado is a robust tree requiring only regular watering and a good mulch in the first years. In very poor or alkaline soils chlorosis can be a problem, as can iron or zinc deficiency. If the tree has been fed with plenty of compost or rotted manure, these should not be a problem.

Harvesting The tree starts to produce fruit within a few years of planting. Fruits can be harvested from October onwards, as soon as they reach a good size. Most do not mature on the tree but rather a few days after being harvested. This makes it possible to stagger the harvest until April or May, taking care to harvest first fruit with skin that shows signs of going dark brown or black. The skin of some varieties turns purplish or becomes lighter in tone when mature. Fruit harvested too early tends to wrinkle and have little taste. When picking, always leave a bit of stalk on the fruit, as otherwise it tends to rot more rapidly.

Problems For the moment, apart from iron or zinc deficiency, excessively saline soil or flooding and compaction of the soil, the cultivation of avocado trees does not pose many difficulties. There have not yet been any pests or diseases detected that cause serious damage. Competition from weeds is easily controlled by mulching until such time as the falling leaves cover the ground and their shade stops weeds germinating.

Cherry

There are many varieties of cherry (*Prunus avium*). There are two main groups producing sour cherries: the 'Morello' cherry mostly grown in Europe and the amarelle type common in the United States. Sweet cherries can also be divided into two groups, the 'Heart' type and the 'Bigarreau' type. Cherries in the first group are heart shaped as opposed to round and have fairly soft flesh. More common with commercial growers – because of their longer shelf life – are the sweet cherries of the 'Bigarreau' type. These are rounder in shape and have crisper, firm-textured flesh. Having a cherry tree or two in the orchard is a pleasure that should not be missed if space is available. Space can be a problem, as they easily reach 10m/33ft high and can occupy an area of 45–50m²/484–538ft².

Climate Cherry trees can grow well in temperate and even cold climates, as long as there are no late frosts or cold pockets in spring. For this reason it is better to plant them in protected sites or on slopes and not at the bottom of valleys or on plains.

Soil There are varieties and rootstocks adapted to all soil types. The most common rootstock for alkaline ground is *Prunus mahaleb*; in siliceous soil wild or common cherry gives good results; in cool, deep, fertile soils the *Prunus cerasus* is normally used.

Watering Apart from regular watering in the first few months after sowing or planting, cherry trees, once established, do not need watering, except in very dry regions or when planted on sandy or stony soil where the water drains away rapidly.

Propagation Although the wild and 'Morello' cherries can be sown from seed or propagated by transplanting the shoots from the bottom of a tree without needing to be grafted, ideally the desired variety is grafted on to one of the rootstocks already mentioned. Grafting can be by shield budding in spring or at the end of July. Crown grafts and grafts with wedge-shaped scions are also used. Using wild cherry as a rootstock produces a dwarf tree. Cuttings can also be used but tend to result in weaker trees.

Planting When planting already grafted trees from a nursery, leave 8–12m/26–40ft between trees, depending on the size reached by the variety chosen.

Pruning Cherry trees are very sensitive to being pruned and tend to react badly, especially to the cutting of thick branches. The central shoot can be pinched out when the tree is 1–1.5m/39in–5ft high to stimulate the growth of various main branches and to make a crown structure. Otherwise cut out only dry branches or ones that are in the way. This is best done just after harvesting the fruit.

Care and maintenance In the first years of the tree's growth it is a good idea to mulch around the trunk to prevent competition from weeds and to keep the soil cool, loose and fertile. Cherry trees produce fruit on small, short branches or spurs that get longer every year. Care needs to be taken when harvesting that these are not damaged.

Harvesting The cherries do not all ripen at the same time, so there is a staggered harvest.

Problems Birds tend to be faster than us at harvesting the fruit. If this becomes too much of a problem it might be worth covering the tree with netting.

Gumming is one of the most serious problems from which cherry trees suffer. You may need to make an incision on the northern side of the trunk to even out the imbalance between the rising and descending sap.

The arrival of aphids, which attack young shoots, is often the result of adding too much nitrogen or excessive watering. In the event of a plague, use a plant-based insecticide. Mediterranean fruit fly larvae may attack the fruit of varieties that mature later when the weather is hot. Use traps containing treacle and natural insecticide or sticky pastes.

Citrus fruits

Some lemons flower and fruit year round.

This family includes sweet oranges (*Citrus sinensis*), bitter oranges (*Citrus aurantium*), mandarins (*Citrus reticulata*), lemons (*Citrus limon*) and grapefruit (*Citrus paradisi*). In Spain, California, Israel, Brazil and Morocco these fruit are often cultivated as vast monocultures. The name *citrus* comes from the Latin word for lemon, which was the first of the citrus family to arrive in Europe (Greece) in about 210 BC. Mandarins came last, arriving from Asia at the beginning of the nineteenth century.

In hot regions it is rare to see a garden or orchard without an orange or lemon tree. These fruit are very popular, most of all for the fact that they mature in the cold season and are plentiful in vitamins, especially vitamin C, so essential for reinforcing the immune system in autumn and winter and helping prevent the onset of colds or flu.

Oranges The most popular of the early maturing oranges is the navel, with its characteristic dimple at one end. Washington navel is an intense orange colour and seedless. Thomson navel is also seedless; lighter in colour, the fruit is smaller and less juicy.

Both are harvested from November. Among the varieties that mature mid-season is the blood orange, which has reddish skin and flesh and is very juicy. It is harvested from January to May. There is also the imperial, a sweet, seedy orange with no acidity that is disappearing from the market despite being ideal for making juice for babies or for people who cannot take acidity.

Among the later maturing varieties is the very juicy and sweet late navel, which is smaller than the other navels and matures between February and April. There is also the salustiana, which has a smooth intense orange skin and is harvested from November until the end of March and keeps well on the tree.

Among the latest maturing varieties are the berna orange, which matures from the end of April and can be harvested till June, and the late Valencia, which is similar but more popular being juicier.

Mandarins The authentic mandarin (or tangerine – the terms are interchangeable) has a strong aroma, fine skin and numerous pips. Sadly it is being displaced (it has even disappeared in many places) by the clementine or satsuma varieties which are bigger with loose skin and seedless. It would appear that seeds are a terrible nuisance to consumers.

Lemons and limes Among the many varieties are the sweet lemons, larger and with edible skin, and the normal-sized, more acidic lemons. Some varieties are harvested in autumn/winter and others flower all year. The year-round varieties are of more interest for the family garden, where what counts is the availability of fruit for regular consumption. Limes are like little green lemons, with a somewhat less sharp flavour. Although very popular in America, they are little known in Europe.

Climate Citrus fruit trees grow in hot climates and do not tolerate either intense cold and frosts or temperatures above 40°C/104°F, so they can be grown only in regions with mild winters and not too hot summers. You may see orange trees in rainy cooler regions but they tend to be ornamental, as the fruit has difficulty maturing: the lack of enough hours of light to synthesize the sugars means that the fruit stays quite acidic. Wind can also be a problem, especially at the time of fruiting, making some kind of windbreak necessary if you do not want to lose the harvest.

Mandarins tend to be more resistant to cold than other citrus fruit. Next in terms of resistance comes bitter orange, followed by sweet orange and lemon.

Soil Citrus trees adapt to almost all soils but prefer one that is neither too loose nor too heavy and is cool, deep and rich in humus.

Watering In regions where rainfall is scarce, the trees need regular watering. Traditionally flood irrigation was used, which involved giving trees a lot of water at spaced intervals. Nowadays drip irrigation has become the norm, often with a program that automatically adjusts the watering according to climatic conditions, sometimes by means of humidity sensors stuck into the ground next to the trees. It is advisable to avoid wetting the trunks of the trees. The roots of citrus trees are very superficial and the trees are likely to suffer if not watered adequately in periods of drought.

Propagation Propagation by means of cuttings or layering is possible, but the way that gives the best results is to sow seeds of bitter orange. When these are two or three years old they are grafted with the desired variety. Seeds that are to be used for sowing should be left in the fruit until you are ready to sow them; once outside the fruit, they dry up and lose their ability to germinate within a few weeks.

In organic gardening healthier and more vigorous trees are obtained by sowing directly in the place where you want the tree to grow. The way to do this is to sow various seeds in a row and then choose the healthiest-looking ones to graft on to. Choose the healthiest ones among the grafted trees, pulling out the others until you are left with 4–5m/13–16ft between trees. The ones you pull out can be transplanted, given away or sold.

The great advantage of citrus is that if you do not like the variety of lemon or orange on any particular

The authentic mandarin is giving way to seedless varieties.

The ripe fruit of the lime remains green.

tree you can always graft a different variety on to it (even if it is an adult tree). You can even transform an orange tree into a lemon or mandarin tree and vice versa. Different varieties can also be grafted on to the one rootstock, so that, for example, one tree has early, mid- and late maturing fruit.

Planting If you opt to plant trees from nurseries that have already been grafted with the desired variety, it is worth buying ones in pots. Bare-root citrus trees, while cheaper, do not give as good results.

Transplanting can be done in spring or autumn, but never in summer or winter. Protect the trunks of young trees from cold and sun by covering them with sackcloth or dark plastic.

Grafting Grafting is usually carried out when the tree is two or three years old, preferably between June and August. This is applicable equally to trees grown from seed and to nursery-grown trees. The normal form of graft is shield or 'T' budding.

Pruning The formation pruning of orange trees and of most citruses is generally aimed at achieving a round or globe shape. Trees can also be pruned in an open-glass shape, which consists of a straight central trunk with slanting branches and numerous twigs on the outside. Pruning for fruit production is generally light and limited to getting rid of dry branches or ones that are crossing each other on the inside of the tree, hindering ventilation. Vertical shoots should also be removed, whether coming out of the trunk or out of the central branches. The best time for pruning citrus is in spring after the fruit has been harvested and just before or at the beginning of flowering. Orange tree prunings with their mass of foliage are traditionally fed to rabbits, sheep and goats.

Maintenance Citrus trees do not need much maintenance if grown in the right climate and in the right kind of soil. In cold climates, where they are sometimes grown as ornamentals, they need taking in or covering in winter. In areas of big production there is a tendency to get rid of weeds by digging or by using chemical herbicides. Both are inadvisable: digging because it damages the roots of the trees, which are very superficial, and herbicides because they leave toxic residues. The best options for weed

control are either to sow a leguminous plant such as clover, cutting it down with a strong lawnmower or strimmer, or a permanent mulch.

Keep an eye on the dampness of the soil. Avoid flooding the trees, as it can produce chlorosis (a condition in which leaves produce insufficient chlorophyll), and be sure to water in dry periods. Mulching reduces watering needs.

To avoid too much acidity building up in the soil, collect fruit that has fallen (as a result of humidity, wind or pests) and throw it on the compost or feed it to rabbits, sheep or goats. Some varieties of clementine suffer from excessive fruit production, to the detriment of size. This can exhaust the tree, causing it to produce fruit only on alternate years. This can be avoided by thinning out the fruit when they are the size of a marble.

Harvesting It is best to harvest oranges, mandarins or lemons when they are fully ripe, as this is when they are at their most exquisite and contain the most vitamins. In commercial production they are usually harvested while still a little green – or even very green – and then gassed with ethylene to change the colour of the skin from green to orange. This fails to get rid of the acidity and sometimes gives them a disagreeable taste. Oranges and mandarins are sensitive to knocks and bumps. These, while not causing them to rot, alter their acids and organoleptic constituents. Commercial production, with its processes of brushing down the fruit, mechanical classification and application of paraffin and fungicides, can easily change the fruit's taste. There is no comparison between an orange picked mature off a tree and the medicinal-tasting, shiny (as a result of paraffin) orange in a shop.

Problems Trees need protection from cold, too much heat and wind. Apart from that, citrus trees do not give many problems, as many varieties are resistant to diseases and pests, especially the Washington navel and most   trees. The serious problems that appear in big monoculture plantations with the specialization of pests and the killing off of natural predators through successive spraying do not occur where trees are grown organically together with other trees or species.

Most fungal diseases, such as root or stalk rot, are caused by too much ambient or soil humidity. This can be avoided by good drainage of heavy or clay soils and also by avoiding excessive nitrogen enrichment – including from natural sources – in periods of prolonged rain. Fruit that are less than 1m/39in from the ground tend to suffer from white rot, but this is not something to be concerned about: simply harvest the bottom fruit first. In intensive farming trees might suffer from degenerative viral diseases, but these are rare in organic production and would appear to be directly related to the imbalance and devitalization of the trees caused by incorrect fertilizing and excessive chemical treatments.

Among the most common pests are snails, which love the leaves, and rodents, which can cause serious damage to the trunks of young trees by gnawing away the bark. Other common parasites are aphids, oystershell scale, woolly aphid, red, white or black louse, orange white fly, fruit fly and citrus leaf miner, the latter a recent serious pest. In organic gardening you do not need to worry about the majority of these if the trees are healthy and well cared for. The pests appear sporadically at certain times of year and are usually kept in check by their natural predators, which are normally present in sufficient numbers in a non-intensive family orchard. When there is a serious plague, spraying with pressurized water using a domestic cleaning machine gives good results. In some situations natural insecticides can be resorted to, although these always have the downside that they can potentially destroy the pests' natural predators. Against the citrus leaf miner there are no known natural predators. However, their reproductive cycle and infestation begin only with the arrival of intense heat, and they attack only the young leaves of the second sprouting, so they do not cause serious loss in production. In young trees they can be problematic. You can protect trees by wrapping them in mosquito netting, if not all year round at least from April and May when the citrus leaf miner is flying around.

Fig

Figs (*Ficus carica*) are robust trees that grow anywhere where there are a few hot months in the year. Although the fruit is considered excessively yin by macrobiotics, who do not recommend eating it, it is thanks to the consumption of dried figs that many Mediterranean villages survived. In some regions dried figs used to provide winter food for humans, rabbits, goats, mules, donkeys and even dogs.

There are many varieties of fig, differing in size and ranging in colour from light green to almost black with tones of violet in between. In precarious, arid conditions fig trees will stay small, whereas in deep, cool soils they can grow to an exaggerated size.

The trees normally produce fruit once a year, from August to October, but in hotter regions they produce an additional early harvest in June/July. These early figs mature on buds of the previous year that have survived the winter.

The roots of fig trees go deep into the earth in search of water and can damage underground cisterns and dry up nearby wells.

Climate Figs prefer hot and temperate climates. They tolerate high temperatures but do not like too much ambient humidity.

Soil They adapt to almost all soils and are not very demanding in nutrients. However, the more deep and fertile the soil the more exuberant the tree, whereas in arid, stony or compacted soils the trees are small and produce little fruit.

Watering Fig trees do not normally require watering and can tolerate very hot summers and prolonged periods of drought. In very dry periods they can be helped with moderate watering, but only outside the period when fruit are ripening. Watering can cause fruit to become watery and open up, leading to early rotting. This frequently happens after summer rainstorms or with the coming of the autumnal rains.

Propagation Fig trees can be propagated by means of seeds, cuttings, layering, or shield or ring budding. They reproduce easily.

Pruning Fig trees develop well without being pruned, although it can be a good idea to pinch out the central bud when the tree is young so that the tree takes on a more oval shape rather than growing too vertically. Pruning for fruit production is done green, by pinching out the ends and thinning fruiting branches. Cutting big branches is bad for the tree and should be avoided. Bear in mind that fruit is produced on both the present year's and the previous year's branches.

Care and maintenance Fig trees require little attention. It is a good idea to keep the area around the trunk free of weeds and avoid too much moisture in the soil, especially in the period of fruit production.

Harvesting One of life's great pleasures is to bite into a ripe juicy fig fresh off the tree. Figs are ripe when a little soft when pressed and, in many varieties, when white cracks appear on the outside of the fruit. To harvest figs out of reach, you can make a special harvesting stick by inserting a stone into the smashed end of a length of cane, pushing the stone down until it gets stuck. The splinters that are left form a kind of receptacle for the fig, which should fall off when you give it a little twist.

Problems Birds tend to be your worst rival at harvest time but other serious problems are unlikely. There might be some oystershell scale and in wet periods some fungi. In very hot regions the insidious Mediterranean fruit fly is possible.

Grape

In the Valencia region of Spain the word for porch is derived from the word for grapevine, so much is a grapevine arbour associated with the front of the house. The grape (*Vitis vinifera*) is a deciduous vine that produces abundant foliage from when it starts sprouting in spring. Cultivated in the form of a pergola on the south side of the house, it provides excellent protection from the sun during the hottest months. Conversely in winter the leaves fall off, thus allowing rays of sun to enter and heat the house. At the same time it provides bunches of grapes that mature at the end of summer, to the delight of children and adults, though not of hungry foxes. According to Aesop's fable, foxes prefer to think the grapes are too green than to admit that they are too high.

The way vines develop lends them to being grown in many forms. Rounded or bushy stocks are normally used in commercial growing for wine, as are horizontal cordons trained along wires. Training the vine up a trellis, or in cold regions growing it as an espalier against a south-facing wall, works well in a family garden. Grapes need long hours of sun and high temperatures in order to ripen well and concentrate the sugars enough to have a sweet, agreeable taste.

Grapes are produced only on new growth; however, not all new growth produces grapes. Nodes with buds subdivide both the main vine and laterals. These buds form into leaves, and more buds sprout between the leaves and the vine. These buds can produce both fruiting shoots and infertile shoots. The buds of fruiting shoots are fatter, softer and squarer than the buds of infertile shoots, which are thin and hard. Fruiting shoots can grow as long as 1m/39in and are very flexible. All this needs to borne in mind when pruning.

Climate Grapes can be grown in many different climates as long as winter temperatures do not fall below −15°C/5°F. Vines grown in the form of an arbour need more sunlight and heat than those grown as vine stocks. Grapes destined for the table need to be sweeter than those destined for wine.

Because grapevines need a certain amount of heat and sunlight hours to develop and mature correctly, in cold regions they are traditionally grown on the steep, south-facing slope of a mountain, the steepness ensuring maximum incidence of sunrays. Growing vines as espaliers against a wall achieves similar results. They cannot take too much ambient humidity, as they are susceptible to downy and powdery mildew. The ideal climate for grapes is rainy winters, dry springs and rain from the middle of July until the end of August with dry weather before and during the harvest.

Soil Grapevines generally grow in most soils, but prefer one that is stony with a coarse texture and is warm and dry with a neutral or slightly acidic pH. They do not do well in compacted, damp soils or in those that are excessively alkaline. Grapes destined for wine do not need much organic fertilizer, whereas climbing vines, because of their greater productivity, need regular doses to keep the soil rich in humus.

Watering Grapevines are drought resistant, but climbing vines need watering in dry periods because of their greater productivity. Be careful not to overwater, as it greatly spoils the quality and sweetness of the grapes.

Propagation Except in some experimental centres, grapes are not propagated from seed. Normally the desired cultivar is grafted on to cuttings of vines that are resistant to phylloxera. This is a type of aphid, originally from America, which devastated European vines at the turn of the twentieth century.

American stocks are resistant to it.

Planting Fruiting shoots, grafted or ungrafted, with plenty of roots are transplanted in much the same way as fruit trees but into smaller and shallower holes. The best time to do this is between the end of winter and beginning of spring.

Grafts The most common forms of grafting are whip-and-tongue, crown and using wedge-shaped scions. The graft is done close to the roots to ensure it stays buried.

Pruning Grape bushes and climbing vines need regular systematic pruning. Without it they develop abundant foliage but no grapes, or only very small ones. Pruning also ensures good air circulation, necessary to prevent moulds and mildews. In the first two or three years prune climbing vines hard, as leaving only a few buds will strengthen the shoots that serve as the central guide of the vine in the future. Winter pruning is done when the plant is dormant: that is, some fifteen days from when the leaves fall off up until about ten days before buds begin to sprout. Pruning green and for fruit production involves a series of processes and is done during the plant's active period. It involves trimming the tops of shoots, suppressing unproductive shoots and suckers, thinning out shoots and bunches of grapes and removing leaves. For this it is worth consulting specialized books or best of all practise with someone who has experience.

Care and maintenance With climbing vines it is enough to weed by hand or better still apply a permanent mulch near the main trunks. The decomposing mulch serves as organic fertilizer. Some well-rotted compost can always be added when renewing the mulch in spring. The thinning out of bunches of grapes as practised in some regions is not necessary if the vines are adequately pruned.

Harvesting The grape harvest is from July to October, depending on variety. The grapes are ripe when they have reached a good size, colour and sweetness. Putting paper bags over the bunches protects them from pests and, up to a point, from ambient humidity, which can induce rotting. If you are planning to make grape juice or wine, it is best to

123

harvest the grapes just before they are fully ripe to avoid them fermenting too rapidly.

Problems Spring frosts, especially late ones, can cause considerable damage to incipient buds. Hailstorms at the end of summer are disastrous and there is little that can be done.

The most common diseases are caused by moulds and mildews. Excessive ambient humidity during hot spells in spring and at the beginning of summer is propitious to both. Bordeaux mixture-based treatments are used to prevent or control mildew. For mould, sprinkle powdered sulphur on the leaves, taking advantage of the morning dew to fix it, or spray with liquid sulphur in the evening.

The roots and bunches of grapes can be affected by other types of rot which are also controlled by applying Bordeaux mixture. Among pests you might come across phylloxera, an aphid-like insect. However, this has stopped being a serious problem since the introduction of rootstocks of resistant varieties from America. On the other hand, the grape moth directly damages the grapes as they mature and it may be necessary to use a plant-based insecticide if it appears. There are other pests, but in organic farming they are rarely a problem; it is better to spend your time pursuing good gardening practices than looking for enemies to battle with.

Kiwi

The kiwi (*Actinidia chinensis*), originally from the shaded undergrowth of forests in China, is a bush with a growth habit similar to that of the grapevine. New Zealanders discovered its great potential as a cultivated plant and promoted its consumption, glorifying its peculiar taste and multiple nutritional qualities – above all its high vitamin content, especially vitamin C. Attempts to grow it in very hot, dry regions have failed, as it needs a certain amount of ambient humidity and prefers cooler climates, such as those found on the north coast of Spain and in some mountainous areas with adequate rainfall. It also needs sufficient light and winters that are not too cold. In other respects it does not require a great deal of care: it just needs regular but not excessive humidity, protection from too much solar radiation, a good dose of compost, a structure to climb up and pruning for fruit production similar to that for grapevines (page 123). Most varieties of kiwi need a male plant for every four or five female plants, or failing that, a male branch grafted on to a female plant.

Climate The best, as mentioned above, is a temperate climate with temperatures of about 25°C/77°F and no heavy frosts in spring. It can tolerate up to −12°C/10°F when in winter dormancy. Too much sun is not good, as it provokes excessive water loss and the kiwi's wide leaves can become dehydrated. Kiwis should also be protected from strong winds, which cause dehydration and can damage the leaves and the rest of the plant. They can be planted in east-facing plots or in the shade of big trees.

Soil Kiwis prefer loose, fertile, sandy soil that does not flood easily. Heavy, clay soils tend to provoke root asphyxiation, while stony, lime soils drain too rapidly, causing the plant to dry out. In both cases a good addition of rotted-down organic matter can partly remedy the problem.

Watering Watering should be regular, preferably by sprinkler, with drip irrigation as a last resort. Flood irrigation is not recommended. In damp, clay soils it is advisable to install good drainage.

Propagation The most common method is by grafting, although kiwis are also easily propagated by cuttings or layering. The seeds of bought fruit nearly always produce male plants, which are fruitless but necessary to pollinate female plants. If you have a friend or neighbour with some good female plants, you can get a branch and graft it on to a male plant grown from seed. Grafting is normally by shield budding, done in September, or by using wedge-shaped scions, at the beginning of March. Already grafted plants can also be bought in specialized nurseries. They are expensive, but four or five females and one male is enough for a family garden.

Planting The ground should have been dug deeply, and a green manure dug in a couple of months before planting is recommended. Dig a hole 60cm/24in deep and 60cm/24in wide and plant the young tree with its root ball, covering it with soil to which has been added some spadefuls of well-broken-down compost or leafmould. Later apply a mulch.

Kiwis are usually planted in rows with 6m/20ft between plants. In big plantations they are planted in rows 4.5–5m/15–16ft apart. If planting only a couple of trees, make sure that they are females and graft a male branch on to one of them to ensure pollination.

Pruning The technique is very similar to that of grapevines. As with grapes, fruit is produced only on the same year's wood. It is enough just to leave some central leaders and prune twice a year (once after harvesting and a second time when all risk of frosts has past). Depending on how vigorous the plants are and how much space is available, you can leave five to eight leaf buds so that the respective fruiting shoots develop. When a branch grows too long and is more

than two or three years old it needs to be cut out and a basal shoot left to grow to replace it.

Care and maintenance The first years are the most difficult, as the plants are extremely sensitive to solar radiation and excessive heat, and in exposed areas need to be shaded in some way. Make sure plants are watered regularly in dry periods and keep plants free of competing weeds. Mulching works well; add to the mulch at the rate that it is absorbed by earthworms and avoid exposing the soil to sun. This works better than hoeing, as the plants' roots are very shallow.

Kiwis being climbers, supports are essential; the stalks can grow 1m/39in or more in a year and grip where they can. The classic support consists of posts 2m/7ft high. A batten is nailed horizontally on to each post at a height of 1.8m/6ft to make the form of a cross. Three or four tensioned cables are hung from batten to batten. The central cable or cables support the main branches of the plant, while the outside cables support the fruiting branches. Other options include a double espalier with three levels 50cm/20in apart, and training the plant over a structure such as a pergola, as is typically done with grapevines. Training a plant this way makes for a very attractive shelter with hairy fruit hanging down but has the disadvantage of over-exposing the leaves to the sun. For the first three years guide the shoots along the supports until the plant is well distributed and harmonious in form. From the third year aim pruning at controlling and developing the plant.

Harvesting The fruit is harvested between November and December. Bear in mind that kiwis continue ripening after they have been picked. In a cool place the fruit keeps well for two or three months and in a fridge, at 1°C/33°F, it can keep for up to five months. Depending on the climate, the fruit can be left on the plant and harvested as it ripens.

Problems For the moment the only known problems are those caused by a soil that is too damp or too dry, too much heat and late spring frosts (kiwis sprout fifteen days before grapevines). No pests other than snails and humans are known and there are no notable diseases.

Loquat

The cultivation and commercialization of loquat (*Eriobotrya japonica*) has greatly increased in recent years. It is undemanding in terms of soil or care and is traditionally found in family orchards, by itself next to the house or on the edges of estates. It has the advantage of producing fruit in spring, thus providing some of the earliest fresh fruit of the year.

Climate As flowers are produced in winter, it requires a hot or temperate climate with no winter frosts.

Soil Loquats grow well in almost all types of soil but prefer one that is neither too acid nor too alkaline.

Propagation Loquats can be easily propagated from seed and although the new tree will not have the same characteristics as the mother tree it will usually produce sweet edible fruit. The desired variety can also be grafted (by shield budding or using wedge-shaped scions) on to quince or loquat seedling rootstocks. The latter option has the advantage of speeding up the initial development and shortening the waiting time until the first fruit is produced. The disadvantage is that the tree stops growing after three or four years and stays at the size reached for the rest of its usually curtailed life.

Care and maintenance Loquats need barely any care. Except in times of prolonged drought or in very hot climates they do not need watering; pruning is also unnecessary, as the tree regulates itself. Nor do loquats suffer much from pests or disease, with the exception of birds and predators of the two-legged long-armed type.

Harvest The fruit is ready to harvest as soon as it has acquired its characteristic yellow colour, shiny or matt depending on variety, and gives slightly when pressed. It is a fruit that needs to be eaten soon after being picked. Luckily the fruit does not ripen all at once and the tree provides a staggered harvest that can last a few weeks.

Medlar

Peach

The common medlar (*Mespilus germanica*) is a bushy tree very similar to quince and ideal for planting in an edible hedge. It produces peculiar, round, brown fruit that open up at the end opposite the stalk in the form of a crown showing the seeds inside. The fruit is bitter and acidic when eaten green and only reaches maturity with the arrival of cold weather in the autumn. The fruit, which appears rotten, is softened by frost and has a sweet flavour and a consistency reminiscent of apple sauce.

Propagation and growing needs are similar to those of quince (page 133) and apple (page 112), to which it is closely related. It is normally grafted on to hawthorn or quince.

There are numerous varieties of peach (*Prunus persica*) with very differing characteristics. There are the round yellow-fleshed peaches, the hard white-fleshed varieties, the flattened *paraguayos* and the popular nectarines. The smooth skin of nectarines is reminiscent of plums, but both the form of the seed and the tree make it clear that they are a variety of peach and share with peaches the type of rootstocks, grafts and care needed.

Peaches are relatively delicate trees and in commercial cultivation barely average ten or twelve years of life. However, in orchards that are well kept in a semi-wild form, say on the edge of a garden or estate, they can live twenty or thirty years. What is certain is that trees are very stressed in conventional cultivation as a result of the intense pruning aimed at getting maximum fruit production. This makes them weak and in need of constant care and attention.

Given the great variety available, with different tastes, textures and harvesting times, it is worth growing more than one peach in your orchard. As trees are small or medium-sized they do not take up too much space.

Climate Peaches, including *fresquillas*, nectarines and *paraguayos*, need temperate and hot climates. They tolerate and benefit from winter frosts and with adequate watering can put up with very hot summers. Spring frosts can be harmful, as peaches tend to flower very early.

Soil Peaches prefer light, fertile soils that are sandy or clay-lime and that are deep and retain enough but not excessive humidity. When grafted on to almond stocks, they tolerate dry, chalky soils, while with plum rootstocks they better tolerate damp soils.

Watering In damp soils and in rainy climates watering is not necessary, but in arid or hot climates peaches need moderate watering in the driest periods. Too much water can lead to a plague of aphids and at the time of fruiting takes away some of the fruits' sweetness and taste.

Propagation Some varieties can be propagated from seed, but in general the species is not stable and it is preferable to graft the chosen variety on to a peach seedling rootstock or on to an almond, plum or apricot rootstock. Using a peach rootstock in loose, cool, deep soils produces long-lived, robust trees.

Bitter almond, and in some cases apricot, is the rootstock most commonly used for growing peaches in dry, chalky soils. It produces vigorous trees, but these are not as long lived as those obtained on peach rootstocks. Plum rootstock is generally used in damp, heavy soils. Transplanting is usually done from autumn onwards in hot regions and in spring in colder regions. Trees are normally planted 4–6m/13–20ft apart, depending on variety and pruning systems.

Pruning Peaches are normally pruned to an open centre, starting from 50cm/20in above the ground. Fruit is formed on one- or two-year-old branches, so pruning has to be well structured to ensure continuity in fruit production. As buds have difficulty forming on old wood, avoid putting the tree out of action through excessive pruning.

The aim in pruning is to substitute a branch that produced fruit for another fruiting branch. With the passing of the years the fruit tends to be produced further and further from the centre of the tree. Pruning of fruiting branches is done in the form of a fishbone, i.e. in one plane removing shoots growing vertically up or down. Also remove alternate shoots and prune back the remaining staggered shoots to two buds. Pruning while green is strongly recommended for all stone fruit to avoid gumming. It consists of thinning and pinching out the terminal bud of fruiting branches.

As the fruit forms, thin peaches to one fruit per cluster and later thin again to leave at least 15cm/6in between fruit.

Care and maintenance It is usual in spring to dig the ground over superficially. However, it is preferable to mulch around the trunks and to sow a green manure or a permanent ground cover, using leguminous plants, in the rest of the orchard. If the mulch is periodically renewed with more organic matter, it is unnecessary to add manure or compost. If instead you opt for removing weeds either mechanically or manually, you need to add some 5–10kg/11–22lb of manure per tree in spring. In dry regions or periods watering should be spaced out and moderate, avoiding flooding the trees.

Harvesting Picking and eating a peach off a tree when it is perfectly ripe is one of the simple pleasures of life. As the fruit does not keep, it is worth growing different varieties in order to stagger the harvest. Fruit can be harvested from a single tree for two to three weeks, starting when the peaches are still a little hard and finishing as they begin to wither, which is when they are at their most honeyed (the Spanish word for peach, *melocoton*, means 'honey wrapped in cotton').

Peaches can also be picked when still a little green and left to mature inside. *Fresquilla* and pavia peaches should be eaten as soon as the peel comes off easily, as they lose much of their flavour when not eaten at their peak of ripeness. Nectarines, once harvested, keep well for quite a few days before spoiling. Hard-fleshed peaches can be made into jam or chutney or conserved in syrup. They can also be cut and dried using a solar dryer (see page 143).

Problems Gumming – a disease that produces a sticky amber sap that comes out through cracks in the branches – is very common in most stone fruit (including cherries, almonds and plums). It appears to be a bacterial attack that starts in one branch and can extend until it affects the whole tree, causing general debilitation and often killing the tree. It can be good idea to cut out the most affected branches with a sharp knife, disinfecting the cuts with propolis tincture and covering them with propolis paste. Disinfect knives or other tools used before using them on other trees.

Cut branches should be burnt immediately. Healthy, vigorous trees growing in suitable fertile soil and that have not been subjected to abusive pruning do not tend to suffer much from gumming.

Peach leaf curl is a fungal disease that causes foliage to curl up and deform, producing blisters that turn different shades of light green, yellow and pink. It is advisable to remove affected leaves and make preventative treatments of Bordeaux mixture in winter (never apply Bordeaux mixture when the tree is in leaf; instead use garlic tincture). Applying nettle tea as a leaf fertilizer reinvigorates the tree and minimizes problems with leaf curl.

Mildew mostly affects the leaves but can also affect young fruit, covering them in a white layer. Powdered sulphur is a good cure. Peach tree borers may attack the trunk or branches; to eliminate them try inserting a flexible bit of wire into the hole. The peach aphid attacks young leaves and buds, causing them to dry up. Make sure that the tree is not receiving too much water or nitrogenous fertilizer and in severe cases spray with plant-based insecticides. Wrapping a sticky or greasy bandage around the trunk prevents ants from transporting the aphids to the young shoots.

The Mediterranean fruit fly is one of the most serious problems for late spring- and summer-maturing fruit. In high-risk areas hang bits of yellow cloth impregnated with sugary treacle and a dilution of plant-based insecticide on the tree. You can also hang inverted bottles from which the bottoms have been cut off, half filling them with cheap diluted fruit juice. The disadvantage of these traps is that they attract beneficial insects as well.

Pear

The large number of varieties of pear (*Pyrus communis*) available makes it possible to choose ones that adapt well to the soil and climate. There are summer-ripening and autumn-ripening pears: if you grow both types you can have a staggered harvest and enjoy the fruit fresh for a long period without having to resort to fruit kept in cold storage rooms or conserves (which tend not to be very tasty). Whether raw or cooked, pears provide an excellent chest tonic and help keep the respiratory passages healthy, especially in autumn, when they are most susceptible to irritation and colds.

Climate Pears prefer temperate, cool climates and tolerate intense cold and winter freezing better than excessive heat and drought. They do well in mountainous areas and are problematic in coastal and very hot regions. As with apples, they need a period of winter dormancy and frosts; the latter control disease and pests, so that the tree buds again in spring with renewed vigour. As this does not happen in hot regions, trees grown there tend to be weaker and live less long.

Soil Pears like deep, fertile soils with a permeable subsoil. They do not tolerate root asphyxiation as a result of soil compaction or flooding. Such conditions can produce chlorosis (yellowing of the leaves). However, there is always the option of grafting your chosen pear variety on to a rootstock that is suitable for the particular terrain.

Watering Watering is only necessary in dry regions or during persistent drought. Avoid flooding the tree.

Propagation Pear trees can be propagated from seed. However, given the genetic variations produced and that the seed must be no more than six months old, the normal practice is to propagate by grafting. The rootstock can be pear sown from seed or grown from pear cuttings. It is also common to graft on to rooted quince or hawthorn cuttings.

Pears grafted on to pear seedling rootstocks need a deep, fertile soil and are more tolerant of drought than of ambient humidity. The trees are vigorous and long lived but have the disadvantage that they do not produce fruit until the sixth or seventh year. Pears grafted on to quince rootstocks do better in cool regions and like light, damp soils, as long as they are not compacted. These trees take fewer years to produce fruit but have the disadvantage of being less resistant and shorter lived than those grafted on to pear seedling rootstock.

When growing pears in alkaline and relatively dry soils, it is a good idea to use a hawthorn rootstock. Although the tree will live only fifteen to twenty years it will bear fruit early. Grafts are normally done by shield budding, but crown grafting is also used. Although quince is the most commonly used rootstock, some varieties of pear do not grow well directly on quince. For this reason a compatible variety is usually grafted on first and then the chosen variety grafted on to it.

Pruning Formation pruning can take whichever form is preferred: open centre or vase, pyramid, column, bush, half-standard, espalier, cordon, etc. When pruning to stimulate new fruiting wood, or maintenance pruning, bear in mind that in the middle part of every branch there are laterals and at the end there are always growth buds. Cutting these back stimulates the production of new buds, which can in turn produce other fruiting formations. This is an interesting task but one that requires great ability and experience on the part of the pruner. It is a good idea to combine cutting back the shoots with bending branches that would naturally grow vertically.

Care and maintenance Pears have similar needs to other fruit trees, especially apple (page 112) and plum (page 131). Mulching works well.

Harvesting The pears are ripe when they change colour and come away easily from the tree on touch. If the pears are to be sold or transported, it is best to pick them before they are completely ripe, as very ripe pears bruise easily.

Problems Excessive humidity either in the soil (which causes chlorosis) or in the air from persistent rain or fog is one of the most worrying problems. Frost and hail can also cause serious harm.

Pear anthracnose is a fungal disease that attacks the branches, leaving dark-grey stains with red borders. The disease deforms the branches and causes them to break easily. Bordeaux mixture can be used as a preventative or curative treatment. Pear canker appears as pustules and patches on the trunk and branches, especially on areas that have been cut. It is usually due to excessive moisture in the soil, making good drainage important. Get rid of all affected parts and treat with Bordeaux mixture.

Pear rust attacks the leaves, so that in a short time they fall off the tree. The fungus is easily recognized, as it makes round, rust-coloured marks on the leaves. The disease needs to be treated with a fair degree of urgency, as the tree can succumb to attack. Gather up and burn the leaves, and make sure that there are no juniper trees near by, as these harbour the fungus over the winter.

Scab is produced by another fungus and can be recognized by the greyish-brown patches on the leaves, branches and fruit. The fruit ends up splitting. Treat preventatively with Bordeaux mixture in autumn.

Another fungus that attacks the fruit is black end, which causes the fruit to turn black and spoil. The only remedy is to pick all affected fruit as quickly as possible to stop the infection spreading.

Among pests there are green shield bugs, which cause little spots and yellow patches on the leaves that end up drying out. Giving a good brushing down to the trunks and main branches and daubing them with clay and lime reduces the problem. In serious cases use a plant-based insecticide. Collect and burn affected leaves.

The codling moth worm is a larva which appears and lays its eggs at the beginning of May. It grows in the fruit pulp, causing fruit to fall before it is ripe. In the event of serious attack, hang pheromone traps and spray preventatively with Bordeaux mixture. Apply the Bordeaux mixture when the tree has finished flowering and another two or three times afterwards every fifteen days. If you have only a few trees it may be worth covering them with antithrip netting during the period when the codling moth is flying around.

The pear weevil, like that which attacks plums, is an insect that gets into the branches, leaves and fruit of the tree. It can be controlled by spraying with plant-based insecticides. The borer grub or worm burrows into the wood, excavating long tunnels. The holes are easily detected, as they exude sap and wood shavings. Use a long bit of fine wire, the end bent into a hook, to extract the worms from the holes. Moths lay eggs on the ground from which hatch larvae that climb up the trunk and devour the leaves, buds and flowers of the tree. They can be controlled by wrapping sticky strips around the trunks. This also stops ants transporting colonies of aphids to young shoots.

Plum

Plums (*Prunus domestica*) are harvested in summer and early autumn, and can be dried or made into jam or conserves. They are very nutritious and somewhat laxative. With so many varieties to choose from, all differing in form, colour, taste and size, you can have various plum trees and enjoy a staggered harvest. They are hardy trees, generally of medium height.

Climate Plum trees are deciduous and tolerate cold winters. However, they do not like late frosts, pockets of cold air or excessive humidity. They prefer climates that are temperate and hot but not too dry.

Soil They are undemanding trees in terms of soil but prefer a medium texture that neither contains too much clay nor is very damp.

Watering They do not need much, but should not be allowed to become thirsty in summer heat.

Propagation Plum trees can be propagated from seed or cuttings or by grafting in spring or mid-August. Propagation by seed is similar to that of apricot (page 114), almond or peach (page 128). The variety 'Claudia' can be grown from seed without suffering much degeneration. Other varieties can be grafted on to a plum seedling rootstock or 'St Julien' plum. A 'Myrobalan' plum rootstock is recommended for lime soils. Grafting plum trees on to bitter almond or peach rootstocks is not recommended, as the trees will be weak. Grafting can be by shield budding, crown or using wedge-shaped scions.

Planting Planting distance for nursery-grown grafted trees is 4–8m/13–26ft, depending on the size reached by the selected varieties.

Pruning It is important to get rid of the shoots that normally sprout at the foot of plum trees, as they can end up smothering the tree or absorbing all the soil nutrients. Plums are bushy trees and it is a good idea to direct growth in the form of horizontal canes by bending the branches and tying them to weights on the ground. Fruit is produced on two-year-old wood, so pruning – if done – should be light. It is often a good idea to pinch out some buds and small fruit to limit production. This stops the tree being exhausted from producing too much (and too small) fruit.

Care and maintenance This is similar to that of apricot, cherry or pear trees (pages 114, 117 and 130).

Harvesting Plums are ripe when they are soft to the touch and come away easily from the tree. If they are for selling fresh, they need to be picked a little before this point, as they spoil easily because of their high water and sugar content. Plums that are to be dried can be left on the tree for a few days after ripening until they start to dry up, to help subsequent dehydration. However, only leave them if there are no enemies in evidence such as birds, wasps, fruit beetles, fruit fly or two-legged long-armed predators. The best jam is made with very ripe fruit.

Problems The plum weevil damages shoots and small fruit. It can be fought off with plant-based insecticides or by shaking the tree to make the larvae fall. Pick these off the ground and destroy.

Aphids can be real addicts of some types of plum and can reach a stage of infestation that destroys the fruit's development. Choose less-susceptible varieties and beware of an excess of nitrogen in the soil or too much watering. In severe cases you can spray with a plant-based insecticide.

Plum rust forms rust-coloured patches under the leaves. It is best to pick off affected leaves and burn them. The tinder fungus destroys the tree's woody tissue. This is a disease similar to that which attacks olive trees and needs tough measures such as cutting out the affected wood or branches. Wounds should be disinfected with iron sulphate solution or propolis tincture. It is a good idea to apply a propolis-based putty as a disinfectant and to help the wound heal.

Pomegranate

The pomegranate (*Punica granatum*), while being a classic fruit of the Mediterranean, is not as popular or well known as, say, oranges or peaches. This is perhaps through laziness, as the peeling and shelling involved requires patience. Once you are over this obstacle, it is a fruit rich in taste and nutritional and therapeutic properties. It has recently been discovered that in addition to its vitamin and high iron content the pomegranate contains a substance of great antibiotic and disinfectant power.

Climate It prefers a temperate climate such as that offered by the Mediterranean coast. In colder and windier climates it should be planted in a south-facing spot protected from the north.

Soil It is not a demanding tree but prefers soils that are deep, fertile and semi-compact. Moist and very compacted soils with a tendency to flood are not recommended.

Propagation Ungrafted trees raised from seed give sour fruit. The commonest form of propagation is from cuttings. Layer cuttings are also sometimes used, as are the shoots that grow around the base of the tree. To use a shoot from the base of a tree, first pile soil on to it and leave it to produce roots before separating it. Sowing seeds directly *in situ* and grafting them a year later by shield budding or using wedge-shaped scions is a good way to get healthy, vigorous trees.

Pruning Pomegranates are not very keen on

being pruned, but as the branches tend to grow in a tangled and irregular manner some initial pruning, normally in an open-glass shape, is often needed. It is also common to let pomegranates grow freely as bushes and the tree fits well in a hedge. It should not be pruned once big, as thick branches have difficulty healing.

Care and maintenance Being robust, the tree does not need any special care. It needs to be watered only in times of serious drought and does not need manure if planted in deep, fertile soil. Applying a mulch for the first few years limits competition from weeds, keeps the soil cool and loose, and provides some nutrients.

Harvesting The earliest pomegranates ripen in September and the harvest continues for a good part of October and in some regions even into November. When the fruit starts to crack open, it should be harvested and kept in boxes of straw to be eaten as required. In the event of strong winds, it is best to harvest the pomegranates earlier and leave them to ripen further in a cool place where the skin will not dry out too fast.

Problems Pomegranates have very few problems apart from those caused by excessive humidity, which can result in a plague of aphids in the young shoots. Rodents can wreck havoc, as they love the fruit. This can be avoided by putting some sort of barrier around the trunks to stop them climbing up.

Quince

Quince trees (*Cydonia vulgaris*) are fast disappearing from orchards, perhaps because the bitter fruit is only eaten as jam. Quince cuttings are often used as rootstocks for grafts of pear or loquat. Trees grown on quince rootstocks develop and fruit in a short time but after a few years stop growing – something that is appreciated in gardens where large trees are not desirable.

Climate Quinces grow in most climates, but prefer a temperate one. Their needs are similar to those of apples, but they are less tolerant of winter cold.

Soil Similar to that required by apples (page 112).

Propagation The most common method is to plant cuttings of the same year's growth. In autumn cut lengths a palm long and bury two-thirds of each in a mixture of sand and very fermented compost. The following year the cuttings can be grafted or transplanted to their final home. Cuttings can be planted directly in their final home if you can be sure they will not dry out.

Care and maintenance Quinces are hardy trees and do not need any special care. They can be pruned in any form, although a bush form is the most usual and allows them to develop how they want.

Harvesting The fruit is left on the tree until it is a pale or intense yellow, depending on variety. It should be harvested before the onset of intense cold and can be kept for some three months without spoiling.

Problems Heavy, moist soils need to be well drained.

...de quien a quien...!

THE GARDEN THROUGH THE YEAR

THE GARDEN IN WINTER

The end of one year and the beginning of the next is a good time to take stock of the garden. Note down what has worked well and what problems you have encountered. This helps when it comes to selecting better plant varieties and finding solutions in order to have better harvests the following year.

It is widely believed that in the cold months of the year the garden is at rest and does not need attention. However, apart from in the coldest and more mountainous regions, the reality is quite different. Where winters are mild and frosts are a rare occurrence, as in much of the Mediterranean region, a garden based on plants that are less demanding of light and heat can continue being productive. Such plants include lettuces, leeks, carrots, beetroot, Swiss chard, artichokes, spinach, broad beans, peas,

In winter there is much less need to water.

radishes, turnips, cabbages, cauliflowers and broccoli. A great advantage of the winter garden is that it needs much less watering.

Clearly solanaceae such as tomatoes, aubergines (eggplants) and peppers, which are great lovers of sun and heat, cannot be grown outside except in southernmost regions. The same is true with plants of the cucurbit family (melons, watermelons, cucumbers and courgettes/zucchini). Apart from needing a lot of sun, these suffer frequent fungal attack when there is too much ambient humidity, as is likely in autumn and winter. However, if you cover tomatoes with plastic to stop rain or night dew from wetting the leaves, you can probably continue harvesting them until the arrival of the first frosts.

Just by growing the winter-tolerant plants in the list above you can have a garden that is in constant activity and provides daily harvests of lettuces and other vegetables. Even in the coldest regions it is possible to harvest nutritious escarole (broad-leaved endive), tasty leeks or therapeutic cabbage. A nightly mulch of straw may be needed, and for lettuces and other more sensitive plants a small plastic tunnel or mini-greenhouse is probably necessary.

Those of you who live in southern coastal regions can have a fairly dynamic garden in winter. Although the rate of growth is much slower than in spring, all the beds can be full of plants. Even so, bear in mind that autumn and winter are periods of withdrawal, which implies centring attention on regenerating the soil. It is a time to feed the soil, dig in well-rotted manure or compost and sow green manures.

The life in the soil does not cease, even in the coldest months, and caring for it should continue. It might be a good idea to remove mulch from beds not in use so that the sun's rays can heat up the soil, albeit minimally. Alternatively, you can keep the beds protected with mulch and best of all is to have a green covering, i.e. a green manure. This should be sown in autumn and can consist of a legume such as vetch, lentils or forage beans mixed with a grass adapted to your climate and soil (oats, rye, etc.). Cut green manures as soon as they show signs of flowering (end of January/February).

Winter is also a good time to plan sowing and other tasks with an eye to the next season. You can prepare protected seedbeds or a hotbed for tomatoes, peppers and aubergines (eggplants).

December tasks

- With a double-handled fork, dig over beds that are free of plants. Spread well-rotted manure or compost over them, preparing them for spring use.
- In colder regions the garden will begin to shut down and harvesting will be reduced to cold-resistant plants: cabbages, Brussels sprouts, leeks, escarole (broad-leaved endive), and spinach. Carrots and lettuces can be harvested from protected beds.
- In the warmest regions the garden will still be very active and you can harvest artichokes, cabbages, broccoli, Brussels sprouts, cauliflowers, escarole (broad-leaved endive), spinach, broad beans, lettuces, potatoes, leeks, beetroot and carrots. Cover beds of carrots sown in August or September with straw to prevent frost damage. You can then harvest these throughout the winter and the beginning of spring.
- In temperate regions sow outside garlic (if not already done), radish, spinach, lamb's lettuce and peas.
- In hot regions towards the end of December you can start preparing a hotbed or protected seedbeds for tomatoes, aubergines (eggplants) and peppers.
- Plant out lettuces, escarole (broad-leaved endive) and leeks.
- This is a good time for making infrastructure repairs – for example, by mending fences, the hen house or any broken tools.
- It is also a good time to take stock of the past year and begin planning the next. Sit down and go over your notes from the year before. Work out a plan for the year ahead, the crop rotations in the beds, sowing, transplanting, etc.

Cabbage is a crop that can be harvested throughout the winter.

January tasks

Now is the moment to start preparing everything, so that when the time comes there are plants to transplant and beds that have been dug and manured.

- It is a good idea to dig holes for trees to be planted in February, leaving the holes open and the excavated soil mixed with compost.
- If it has been a good year and you have planned your sowing and transplanting well, you can harvest Swiss chard, artichokes, broccoli, escarole (broad-leaved endive), spinach, cabbage, cauliflower, broad beans, lettuces, turnips, leeks, radishes . . .
- In the warmest regions sow tomatoes, aubergines (eggplants), courgettes (zucchini) and perhaps peppers in a hotbed.
- In a protected seedbed sow leeks, escarole (broad-leaved endive), lettuces and spring cabbage.
- Sow directly outside garlic and radishes, and in warm regions, early carrots.
- Spread compost around fruit trees and vines, pushing aside the mulch. Leave the mulch off until the spring sun is properly hot.
- Consult the lunar calendar for good days for planting fruit trees.
- Except where there is still risk of heavy frost, finish pruning fruit trees. Consult the lunar calendar for the best days to prune. In the warmest regions start pruning orange trees; in colder regions leave it until Easter.

137

February tasks

Intense cold continues and in many regions night frosts keep the garden at a standstill until the end of the month or the beginning of March. In most regions only plants started off in a hotbed will be growing. In the warmest regions some of these plants can be pricked out and transplanted to containers in the open air or under cover. This way the plants will put down good roots and harden off, ready for transplanting outside.

- Harvest Swiss chard, artichokes, broad beans, spinach, escarole (broad-leaved endive), lettuce, turnips, leeks, radishes . . .
- In temperate regions artichokes begin sprouting a second time and can be harvested right up until early spring.
- Sow in a hotbed aubergines (eggplants), cabbages, cucumbers, tomatoes and peppers.
- Sow under cover Swiss chard, escarole (broad-leaved endive), lettuces and leeks.
- Sow in the open air radishes and beetroot. In the warmest regions sow carrots and green beans.
- Sowing or transplanting under protection, using tunnels or plastic covers, can bring forward some cold-sensitive plants such as tomatoes or green beans.
- In some regions it may be a good time to dig in green manures sown at the beginning of autumn.
- Fruit trees: the time for planting trees that drop their leaves is coming to an end. Olive and hazelnut trees can be planted.
- Finish the pruning of fruit trees, as long as there is no more risk of heavy frost. Prune if possible in a waning moon.

THE GARDEN IN SPRING

The rigours of winter are now more or less over and everywhere nature is beginning to show signs of transformation as the pulse of spring quickens. At this time of year everything happens very quickly: the gardener cannot afford to be lazy and must shake off the lethargy of winter.

The garden has started to wake up and in spite of the odd late frost or rainy day there are plenty of days of spring sunshine in which to enjoy making new beds and sowing or transplanting into those prepared in winter.

There may be some beds of green manure (vetch or forage beans) flowering at this time. This is a sign that it is time to cut the plants down and leave them to decompose on the surface for a while. When they show some degree of dehydration, work them lightly into the soil. After cutting down the green manure you can spread some compost on the bed: 1–4kg/2–9lb per $1m^2/11ft^2$ (depending on what crop is planned) .

It is a good idea to plant tomatoes, peppers, aubergines (eggplants) and even cabbages and lettuces directly into these beds (where the cut-down green manure and compost has been left on the surface or lightly mixed with the soil). Over time the decomposing roots of the green manure contribute a large quantity of nutrients such as nitrogen, synthesized by the nitrogen-fixing bacteria in legumes.

It is time to think about mulching. Consider covering those beds that were previously left uncovered to get a bit of winter sunshine. With the increase in temperatures there is more likelihood of weeds germinating. The darkness provided by the shade of a mulch of straw or other organic material stops germination and thus saves hours of weeding later. Beds that are to be sown directly with carrots, runner beans, etc. are of course left unmulched. However, covering them with a finger depth of leafmould or very mature compost serves various functions: it maintains the moisture necessary for germination, it accumulates the sun´s radiation (being dark in colour), it lightly protects the soil from the cold at night and it inhibits the germination of competing weeds.

The blossom of fruit trees brightens the spring garden.

In cold regions it is time to plan sowings and other tasks with an eye to the coming season. It is a good idea to make a start on protected seedbeds and a hotbed for tomatoes, peppers and aubergines (eggplants).

In fact in most regions either under protection or in the open you can sow lettuces, carrots, cabbages, Swiss chard, beetroot, turnips, radishes and spinach. In warm and temperate zones you might risk sowing dwarf beans and courgettes (zucchini). Melons and watermelons can be sown under cover.

Once the risk of frost has past, tomatoes, aubergines (eggplants), peppers, courgettes (zucchini) and squash can be transplanted outside. Melons and watermelons can be transplanted in April or May.

Keep an eye on protected seedbeds and green-houses. On hot days they need to be opened up and ventilated, and on cold days and at night they need to be closed. If it is very cold, cover them with a blanket or matting, remembering to remove it when the sun comes up.

Make the most of the phase of full moon (or descending moon) to turn compost piles that were made in autumn or winter. You can improve the composition of the compost by adding wood ash or lime if you have an acid soil, or porous sand (perlite or vermiculite) or coconut fibre if you have a clay, compacted or very heavy soil.

March tasks

The soil, gardens and fields all fill with life as the month progresses, building up to an explosion of light and

Radishes are quick-growing crops.

greenery. This is followed in the months to come by a multicolour display of flowers. Nevertheless, March is a changeable month; spring is beginning but winter can return unexpectedly. It is usually a critical time in the garden: the sharp contrasts can cause a certain stress to cultivated plants and lay them open to pest attack.

- Harvest artichokes, all types of cabbages, cauliflowers, escarole (broad-leaved endive), spinach, peas, broad beans, lettuces, leeks, radishes and carrots.
- It is possible to sow and plant practically everything, except in colder regions. Although the days are getting longer, time and hands are normally lacking to do all that you might wish. Between preparing beds, sowing and transplanting there is little free time.
- Keep an eye on the ventilation of protected seedbeds, tunnels and greenhouses.
- In a protected seedbed sow aubergines (eggplants), squash, melons, cucumbers, peppers and tomatoes.
- In an open seedbed sow Swiss chard, asparagus, broad beans, beetroot, carrots, celery, parsley, lettuces, and Lombard and summer varieties of cabbage.
- Transplant spring cauliflower and leeks. In hot regions begin transplanting early tomatoes and courgettes (zucchini) to the open air but with protection (e.g. plastic water containers with the base cut off). You might risk transplanting peppers, aubergines and cucumbers.
- In hot regions grafting of fruit trees of the stone type (peach, plum, etc.) can begin.

April tasks

In most regions April is the month of transplanting, as the risk of frost is almost over.

- A late blast of cold can cause a lot of damage to many plants that are already at an advanced stage of growth. Be ready to protect sensitive plants such as tomatoes and courgettes (zucchini) at the slightest indication of an overall drop in temperature.
- April can also bring fierce heat; make sure protected seedbeds, tunnels and greenhouses are ventilated. Too much heat can be very harmful at this time.
- Make the most of the abundance of nettles to make nettle tea. Use this to stimulate the healthy development of leaf plants (Swiss chard, lettuces) and reinforce the defences of other plants.
- Harvest cabbage, escarole (broad-leaved endive),

Unmulched beds need hoeing, weeding and earthing up.

spinach, peas, broad beans, lettuces, turnips, leeks, beetroot, radishes and carrots. In hot regions, also strawberries.

- In a protected seedbed sow squash, courgettes (zucchini), melons, cucumbers, peppers and tomatoes.
- In an unprotected seedbed sow Swiss chard, celery, cabbages and lettuces.
- Sow directly parsnips, spinach, green beans, sweetcorn, turnips, radishes, beetroot and carrots.
- Plant out onions, cabbages, lettuces and tomatoes, and (but with protection) peppers, aubergines (eggplants) and courgettes (zucchini).
- Hoe and weed the beds or put a mulch around plants that were sown or transplanted last month.
- If necessary nip the outside shoots of tomatoes and train tomatoes and climbing beans up supports.

May tasks

The garden is usually looking exuberantly green. It is time to finish sowing and planting for harvesting in summer and autumn.

- In unmulched beds hoeing, weeding and earthing up follow on from each other. The soil has started to heat up and it is worth building up the mulch on mulched beds to avoid weeding and minimize watering.
- Staggered sowing and transplanting of lettuces, courgettes (zucchini), cabbages and radishes avoids a gap in the harvest.
- In many regions May is the best month for sowing sweetcorn (corn). Sweetcorn for eating raw is best sown at fifteen-day intervals, given the short time that the cobs are at their best.
- Harvest young garlic, celery, Swiss chard, white

Green pruning

Although traditionally deciduous trees are pruned during winter dormancy, this may not in fact be the best thing for their health and vitality. A branch of some thickness cut in winter will heal badly and the cut will be an entry point for disease. If you plan ahead and know how you want the tree to develop, you can pinch out or cut branches of no interest when they are still small and this way the tree suffers far less damage. When the tree is in active growth its sap secretes antiseptic and healing substances. For this reason spring or summer green pruning is best. The ideal moment to prune is after the fruit has been harvested, as fruit trees are used to suffering damage and broken branches at the time of fruiting and harvest.

Choosing when to prune according to the moon both improves the results and helps the cut to heal. The moon calendar (see page 49) is useful for this. Choose a 'fruit' day when the moon is descending, if possible coinciding with its waning. This way future fruit production is stimulated and the bleeding out of sap avoided.

onions, broccoli, cauliflower, asparagus, spinach, peas, lettuces, turnips, leeks, radishes and carrots. In hot regions harvest courgettes (zucchini), green beans and cucumbers.

- Sow in the open or in seedbeds courgettes (zucchini), cabbages, Brussels sprouts, summer and autumn cauliflowers, lettuces, melons, cucumbers and leeks.
- Sow directly courgettes (zucchini), squash, cabbages, escarole (broad-leaved endive), spinach, dwarf and climbing beans, lettuces, melons, cucumbers, radishes, beetroot, carrots and (in cold regions) peas.
- Transplant aubergines (eggplants), squash, onions, cabbages, cauliflowers, melons, peppers, leeks, tomatoes and courgettes (zucchini).

THE GARDEN IN SUMMER

With the good weather and longer days the garden is probably overflowing and producing more than you can eat. It is also time to say goodbye to some plants that are more sensitive to heat such as broad beans, peas and spinach, but as there are so many others to harvest that is not such a hardship.

Monitor the watering High summer temperatures and the usual scarcity of rainfall make watering a priority at this time. In high summer it is best not to water during the day with any method that wets the plants (that is using a sprinkler, hosepipe or watering can). A drip irrigation system is ideal, as it moderates the temperature of the soil without wetting the plants. Mulch also keeps the ground from overheating and is the best practice in summer.

You might well be going away for a week or two in this season, in which case you need to find a way

Plants require a reliable supply of water throughout the summer.

for the garden to continue to be watered in this critical time. Ask help from a neighbour, family or a friend – maybe someone to whom you give a basket of fresh vegetables from time to time. If you are lucky enough to have a programmed localized drip irrigation system, you need to check the whole system, looking for any bad connections or breaks. It is still worth asking someone to check the garden from time to time.

Abundant harvests It is important to choose the best moment to harvest, leaving aside those vegetables and fruits destined for seed. Try to harvest as soon as the vegetable or fruit is mature, even if you are not able to eat it. Leaving fruit to rot on the plant can lead to the rest spoiling, as often happens with tomatoes. Also, when fruits are left to develop too much the plants believe they have already secured descendants. When seeds are left to develop in mature courgettes (zucchini), beans, aubergines (eggplants) and peppers, the plants stop developing or even flowering, or the flowers fall without setting. Therefore to have a continuous harvest it is best to pick all mature or fully developed fruit as well as any vegetables going to seed – lettuces, cabbages, radishes, carrots. These can be cut up and put on the compost heap or fed to the chickens.

The problem at this time of year is often what to do with an abundance of tomatoes, peppers, aubergines (eggplants), courgettes (zucchini), etc. If the list of family and friends who would gratefully accept your surplus is short, or many of them are away on holiday, the best thing to do is to process the surplus and fill the larder for winter. A solar dryer (see box) makes it possible to dehydrate most vegetables and fruit, previously cut up into slices. Sealed hermetically in glass jars, these will last a long time. To use them, simply soak in water for a few hours and then cook as normal. Preserving in glass jars is traditional and one of the easiest ways of conserving. The jars can be recycled, but it is best to buy new lids every year to ensure a good seal. Cabbages, beetroot, carrots and other root vegetables can be preserved using lacto-fermentation, producing sauerkraut. This method, as well as preserving vitamins and mineral salts, contributes additional nutritional and therapeutic properties. Branches of 'hanging' varieties of tomatoes can be cut down and hung up in a dry place and consumed fresh throughout the winter. Green beans and sweetcorn (corn) can be frozen and eaten as autumn sets in.

Summer tasks When the summer heat intensifies, it may be advisable to whitewash the greenhouse or cover it with shade netting. This both protects the plastic from degrading and prevents the ground inside from heating up excessively and destroying the microbial life.

The orchard With the arrival of the hot weather a lot of insects appear. Many of these are undesirable in fruit trees, such as aphids, fruit flies, etc. Prepare sticky traps and mosquito nets to have ready when needed. Traps are also useful for identifying garden pests.

June tasks

- It is very likely that the heat will be so intense that you will need to increase watering considerably, especially of plants such as courgettes (zucchini), Swiss chard, lettuces, escarole (broad-leaved endive), tomatoes, etc.
- Competitive weeds are at their most vigorous, so do not ignore hoeing and most of all mulching. Mulching where appropriate will save you many hours of weeding and reduce the watering necessary.
- Beds that were occupied with winter crops and some spring crops can be freed for use. Compost heaps welcome the remains of harvests.

Solar dryer

A solar dryer uses convection currents to move solar-heated air past trays of vegetables or fruit carrying moisture away. The vegetables/fruit, which have been cut into slices, can be preserved in sealed glass jars. To use, simply put the vegetables/fruit in water for a few hours first.

The solar dryer is a simple design and makes for a better-quality product than drying in direct sunlight, as ultraviolet rays can partially destroy valuable nutrients.

Remove weeds, which compete with plants for nutrients and water.

- It is a good idea to weed strawberry plants and re-move runners. Watering them more frequently can extend yields for a good while longer.
- Melons and watermelons will be starting to form. Prune back some lateral shoots to help the fruit develop.
- Continue pruning lateral shoots of tomato plants and tying the main stalk to cane supports.
- Harvest Swiss chard, celery, courgettes (zucchini), onions, cauliflowers, spinach (the last in warm and temperate regions), strawberries, peas (possibly only in cold regions), broad beans (in cold regions), green beans, lettuces, turnips, potatoes, leeks, rad-ishes, tomatoes (in hot and temperate regions), car-rots, beetroot . . .
- Sow in an unprotected seedbed autumn and winter cabbages and cauliflowers, escarole (broad-leaved endive) and lettuces.
- Sow *in situ* dwarf and climbing beans, courgettes, sweetcorn (until the middle of the month), parsley, radishes, beetroot and carrots.
- Transplant celery, onions, cabbages, cauliflowers, lettuces, leeks and late tomatoes in hot regions.

July tasks

The good weather, light and heat make July a month of abundant harvests. Be prepared for a surplus of vegetables and think about what to do with them; you will probably have lots to give away to family, friends and neighbours.
- Select which tomato, aubergine (eggplant), pepper

and bean plants are to be left to go to seed. Give maximum care to those chosen for seed saving, in terms of watering, earthing up and removing pests. This way you obtain good-quality seeds.
- Prune side shoots growing between the main stem and the leaves of tomato plants to improve fruiting. Courgettes (zucchini), cucumbers, melons, watermelons, aubergines (eggplants) and peppers can also be pruned to help fruit development by cutting back the main stem or stems.
- No doubt there are areas of the garden where weeding has been neglected. Pull up weeds now before they produce seed and throw them on the compost heap.
- Continue monitoring fruit trees and fruit for pests. Above all, watch out for the Mediterranean fruit fly, which can ruin the harvest.
- Harvest Swiss chard, celery, aubergines (eggplants), courgettes (zucchini), cabbages, parsnips, escarole (broad-leaved endive), fennel, green and dry beans, lettuces, sweetcorn (corn), turnips, cucumbers, peppers, leeks, radishes, beetroot, tomatoes and carrots.
- In cold and humid regions it is still possible to harvest artichokes, spinach, peas and broad beans.
- Sow *in situ* Swiss chard, escarole, spinach (in cold and temperate regions), turnips, lettuces and radishes.
- Plant out celery, cabbages, Brussels sprouts, autumn cauliflowers, lettuces and late tomatoes.
- From mid-July start transplanting artichoke shoots.

Pinch out side shoots of tomatoes to encourage fruiting.

August tasks

The first fortnight of August can be really suffocating. In Mediterranean regions from the middle of the month expect some refreshing summer storms.

- Continue attending to watering, mulching and weeding.
- It is important not to ignore harvesting and to pick fruit and vegetables at the right stage of their development. Check courgettes (zucchini) daily, tomatoes every two or three days at least, green beans every three or four days, and peppers and aubergines (eggplants) every five or six days at the minimum.
- Now is the time to enjoy the sweet refreshing taste of melons and watermelons.
- Harvest practically everything: Swiss chard, celery, watercress, aubergines (eggplants), onions, cabbages, summer cauliflowers, escarole (broad-leaved endive), lettuces, melons, potatoes (in cold regions), cucumbers, peppers, leeks, radishes, watermelons, tomatoes and carrots.
- Sow in an unprotected seedbed onions, cabbages and lettuces.
- Sow *in situ* Swiss chard, borage, escarole (broad-leaved endive), lettuces and turnips.
- In temperate regions potatoes can be planted for harvesting in October or November.
- Plant out broccoli, autumn cauliflowers, leeks and artichokes, and transplant strawberry shoots.
- In hot and in some temperate regions it is time to plant out late tomatoes.

THE GARDEN IN AUTUMN

Brown and ochre hues begin to predominate in the garden, reminding you that autumn is the transition to the cold of winter. Garden activity slows down in most regions and nights are longer, robbing hours of light from the day. In spite of the slowdown in plant growth, autumn harvests are abundant and varied in many gardens. In temperate regions you can still harvest green beans, tomatoes, courgettes (zucchini), aubergines (eggplants)and peppers as well as vegetables that are harvested almost year round, such as lettuces, carrots, Swiss chard, celery, cabbages, Brussels sprouts, radishes, beetroot and parsley.

In autumn there may be some special harvests such as peas, leeks, spinach and escarole (broad-leaved endive). Potatoes can be dug up as needed for the table or stored in a cool dark place after a good airing.

In cold regions there is the possibility of early frosts. Sensitive plants that are still producing fruit, such as tomatoes, peppers and aubergines (eggplants), need to be covered with a straw mulch or plastic.

Autumn tasks Beds now free of summer harvests can be cleaned up and made ready for autumn crops – cabbages, cauliflowers, escarole (broad-leaved endive), broad beans, spinach, etc. – and for spring sowing and planting – peas, Swiss chard, leeks, etc. In beds that are not put to use you can sow green manures such as vetch and forage beans. These grow into big clumps and can be cut down in February or early March as flowering begins, leaving welcome nutritious beds for tomatoes, peppers or aubergines (eggplants). As sunlight hours decrease, remove the straw mulch from the base of tomato plants. This gives the dark compost a chance to absorb the solar radiation and warm the roots, without which the tomatoes will not mature.

Prevent fungus attack Spraying plants with a concoction of horsetail, or horsetail and nettle tea, every fifteen days provides them with an effect similar to that of light, which is becoming scarce. The silica contained in horsetail reinforces the plants and a periodic application protects plants from rot, fungus

145

attack and diseases such as mildew and mould. Covering tomato plants that are still producing fruit with plastic protects leaves from rain. This prevents mildew developing and makes it possible to harvest tomatoes until the beginning of winter.

The orchard Autumn fruits, rich in vitamin C, help to boost our resistance to the brusque temperature changes that characterize autumn. Harvesting begins of apples and pomegranates. Next come the first mandarins, clementines and oranges; these continue throughout autumn and winter. In some regions kiwis are ready to be harvested.

September tasks

September is a changeable month: it can be hot, a continuation of summer, or a prelude to autumn with copious rain and cold gusts.

- From September green manures can be sown

where demanding crops – tomatoes, aubergines eggplants), potatoes – are to be planted.

- In some regions it is a good idea to prune the main stalks of tomato plants. This helps concentrate energy in the fruit so that it matures before the arrival of cold weather.

- In temperate regions artichokes are in their first stages of development. They need to be given a lot of attention, most of all in terms of careful hoeing.

- Now is the ideal time to organize getting manure and to prepare compost with a view to digging it in at the end of autumn or beginning of spring.

- Harvest Swiss chard, celery, aubergines (eggplants), onions, cabbages, cauliflowers, escarole (broad-leaved endive), lettuces, melons, potatoes (in cold regions), cucumbers, peppers, leeks, radishes, watermelons, tomatoes and carrots.

- Sow Swiss chard, celery, cabbages, asparagus,

spinach, peas, escarole (broad-leaved endive), leeks, lettuces, radishes, turnips, fennel . . . On warm coasts it is a good time to sow broad beans.

- Plant out onions, cabbages, cauliflowers, lettuces, escarole (broad-leaved endive), leeks. In hotter regions it is still possible to plant artichoke offsets.

October tasks

- October can be cold, with copious rainfall. Colder regions might suffer the first frosts. Try to harvest more sensitive crops and protect those left in the soil.
- More sensitive plants can be treated with horsetail to prevent fungus attack.
- Continue sowing green manures in free beds.
- In most gardens harvests continue to be plentiful. Harvest Swiss chard, celery, squash, Brussels sprouts, cabbages, escarole (broad-leaved endive), lettuces, spinach, peas, parsley, leeks, beetroot, carrots . . .
- In temperate regions you can still harvest green beans, tomatoes, courgettes (zucchini), melons (the last ones), aubergines (eggplants), peppers (also the last) and sweetcorn (corn). Artichokes may be coming into flower.
- Sowing is now reduced. It is still possible to sow outside spinach, garlic, peas, broad beans, lettuces, potatoes, radishes and leeks.
- Plant out onions, spring cabbages, lettuces, leeks, escarole (broad-leaved endive), Swiss chard and strawberry suckers.

November tasks

- In November the proximity of winter can be felt and it is advisable to harvest or pull up any sensitive plants still left in the garden. Plants that are left in the ground all winter, such as carrots and leeks, can be covered with straw. This stops the ground from freezing and keeps it soft, making it easier to pull up plants later.
- On the other hand it is a good idea to take away the mulch from around most other plants, such as cabbages and lettuces. Weeds are no longer such a problem; nor is it so important to retain moisture in

the ground. Uncovering the soil exposes it to light and enables it to accumulate some heat, which is always appreciated by plants.

- It is important not to leave crop remains in the beds. Pull up and add to the compost heap, and cover with a layer of dry leaves.
- In hot regions it is still possible to sow green manures in empty beds.
- It is a good idea to start spreading manure around fruit trees. Leave it on the surface for a while and from January/February onwards cover it with mulch or dig it in superficially.
- Harvest Swiss chard, artichokes, celery, various types of cabbages, Brussels sprouts, pak choi, cauliflowers, spinach, peas, fennel, turnips, parsley, leeks, radishes, beetroot and carrots. In temperate regions harvest aubergines (eggplants), courgettes (zucchini) and tomatoes.
- Sow *in situ* garlic, spinach, escarole (broad-leaved endive), broad beans, lettuces, potatoes and radishes.

Protecting tree trunks

After a vigorous brushing down, daub tree trunks with a mixture of clay, lime, wood ash and powdered milk. This provides the best protection against pests and leaves them to pass the autumn and winter in the best conditions possible.

Trunk treatment against pests.

APPENDIX 1: SEED SAVING

Most seeds can be kept for years without losing their vitality or ability to germinate. Some such as green bean seeds should not be kept for more than two years, while others such as lettuce keep well for six to eight years. It is best to keep seeds in a cool, dark, dry place such as glass jars with hermetically sealing tops in the bottom of the fridge. In the jar put a piece of paper with the name and variety of the plant, year of harvest, perhaps the plot it was harvested from and any additional notes on its characteristics (e.g. good taste, resistant to mildew, etc). A little bag of silica granules or a piece of chalk can be put inside the jar to absorb any excess humidity.

Saving seeds from commonly grown vegetables

Swiss chard, lettuces, cabbages, escarole, carrots, onions, leeks Having selected the best plants for seed, leave them to go to seed. To prevent the seeds of escarole, lettuce, celery or Swiss chard being eaten by birds or blown away by the wind, put a fine mesh such as mosquito net over the flowers. Pull the plants up when they are completely dry and hang them in an airy, dry, covered area to finish drying. At midday on a dry, sunny day spread the plant out on a big piece of cloth and hit it with a stick until all the flowers have come off. Then blow on the pile of seeds so that the lighter fragments blow away and the seeds stay at the bottom. Clean and select the seeds manually and put in a glass jar.

Cabbages, cauliflowers, broccoli, radishes and turnips The crucifer family develop pods after flowering in which the seeds form. Cover the flowers with mesh when you can see the pods beginning to form and leave them to develop and dry out on the plant. When the pods start opening, cut down the plant and hang it under cover until it finishes drying. On a dry, sunny day extract the tiny seeds from the dry pods by hand and collect those that fell into the mesh when the pods opened.

Tomatoes Choose the best tomatoes from the healthiest, most vigorous plants that ripen first. Leave them to mature on the plant and after harvesting them (during a full moon) leave them to mature further until they start to dry up.

When there is a full moon remove the seeds by rubbing the tomatoes cut in two on a piece of cotton or sackcloth, or on a paper napkin. Leave this to dry well in the sun. Alternatively put the cut-up tomatoes in a bucket of water until the seeds separate from the pulp. Leave the seeds and the pulp in the water for a few days until they start fermenting (this helps to clean the seeds). The healthy seeds will be heavier than the water and will stay at the bottom, while the pulp and the unhealthy seeds will stay suspended in the water. Pour out the water carefully until only the seeds remain in the bucket. Put the seeds on a piece of cotton or sackcloth and leave to dry in the sun for three days to a week, covering them at night. Once they are properly dry they can be kept in a glass jar with a bit of chalk or silica.

Aubergines (eggplants) Leave the aubergines selected for seed to mature fully on the plant (they go yellow and then brown).

Harvest them during a full moon and leave them in the sun for a few weeks until they are well dried or begin to spoil. Cut them up and pull them apart in a bucket of water and continue as for tomatoes.

Peppers Leave the best peppers on the healthiest plants to dry well on the plant. Then harvest and leave in the sun for a few days until they are shrivelled up. Open up the peppers and take out the seeds, leaving them to dry out completely in the sun for a few days more before putting them in a glass jar.

Courgettes (zucchini) and cucumbers The courgettes and cucumbers that are not harvested swell up on the plant and finally turn completely yellow. At this stage they can be picked and left in a place protected from the sun for a few weeks so that they can finish maturing and forming seeds. When they start to look bad, cut them up and put in water, clean the seeds and follow the same procedure as for tomatoes.

Melons and watermelons After eating a melon that has grown well and has a good flavour, collect the seeds on a plate or on a piece of sackcloth and leave them in a dry, airy, sunny place. When they have dried out, fold them in the sackcloth, put them in a glass jar and store in a dry, cool place.

Green beans, broad beans, peas and seeds of other leguminous plants From when pod production starts, leave unharvested some pods from the plants that have grown the most vigorously, so that they form seeds. During a full moon and when they are completely dry, pull up the plants and hang them under cover to finish drying. At midday on a dry, sunny day remove the seeds, separating them from the other dead plant matter by blowing. Keep the seeds in glass jars to which have been added cut up bits of dehydrated garlic or seeds from the castor oil plant to protect the seeds from weevils.

Potatoes Keep potatoes that are to be used for sowing in a cool, dark place. Ideally they should be stored in boxes in layers, with each layer completely covered with a mixture of coconut fibre and sand. This way they are kept dry and dark but maintain their humidity and are less likely to send up early shoots. If clematis grows in the vicinity hang a few plants of it around the box of potatoes (or pile, if you are storing them in a pile). Clematis has an insecticide and repellent effect and prevents potatoes getting destroyed by potato moth.

APPENDIX 2: PESTS AND DISEASES

In the words of Jesus Arnau, 'The question of plagues should be seen not as a pub brawl but as a game of chess.'

As mentioned before, it is far better to spend your time pursuing good gardening practices than looking for enemies to battle with. However, below is some practical advice on how to combat the most common pests and diseases.

Ants

Copper rods or metal mesh pyramids can be put over the entrance hole to ants' nests. Ants choose places with certain telluric energies when making their nests and if the energy is altered they look for a more suitable place to live. Nasturtiums, lavender and chopped-up bay leaves repel some types of ant.

Aphids

Aphids are sucking insects that need much more nitrogen than carbohydrates for their development. This means that they filter the sap of plants and excrete a sticky treacle-like substance on the leaves. This substance is food for ants, which then take charge of transporting the aphids to the tenderest shoots, which are richest in nitrogen. Black sooty mould tends to proliferate on the treacly substance. By stopping light reaching the leaves the fungus ends up weakening the plant because photosynthesis cannot take place. In general aphids appear during periods of rapid growth in crops, especially in soils that have been enriched with a lot of nitrogen. Their presence tends to be very seasonal and often a change in the weather will be enough to make them appear or disappear.

If aphids turn into a real problem, treating affected plants with potassium soap (100g/3½oz of soap diluted in 10 litres/2½ gallons of water) is enough to get rid of them. Only in extreme cases of great resistance or persistence is it advisable to resort to the use of natural wide-spectrum insecticides such as pyrethrum.

Hoverfly larvae, ladybirds and their larvae, earwigs and green lacewings all feed off aphids.

Caterpillars and maggots

Most caterpillars and maggots are easy to remove manually. If you are faced with a massive attack, *Bacillus thuringiensis* is very effective. These bacteria feed on lepidoptera larvae, paralysing the digestive system. It is a good idea to make regular preventative treatments at sundown (ultraviolet radiation destroys the bacteria).

Codling moths

Pheromone traps are used in the control of codling moths, which lay their eggs in fruit, especially pip fruit such as apples and pears. Another method of control is to wrap raffia, sackcloth or corrugated cardboard around the trunks and main branches of the fruit trees. The caterpillars hide underneath and can be removed manually. Preventative treatments with fermented extracts of wormwood and comfrey have a repellent effect, as codling moths do not lay their eggs in the treated trees.

Earwigs

Although earwigs sometimes feed on tender leaves, any damage is insignificant compared to the benefits they bring, as their basic food is aphids. Some farmers go so far as to put flowerpots filled with dead leaves or straw upside down on a stick to provide them with a refuge by day so that they will devour aphids by night.

Fungal diseases

The appearance of damaging fungi is normally caused by a loss of equilibrium in the plant, related to humidity. Possible factors include the siting of the plants, plant adaptation, pruning or high temperatures and humidity. It can also arise from having fed excessive nitrogen to the soil or plants. The nitrogen forces the plants to absorb water in abnormal quantities, creating favourable conditions for parasitic fungi.

Powdery mildew This shows itself as a whitish floury bloom on the leaves and stalks of weak plants, and is most commonly found in shady areas and in regions or periods of high humidity. Its effect is to dry out the leaves. Sometimes just exposing the plant to the sun is enough to kill off the mildew. Mildew is common on the leaves of cucurbits such as courgettes (zucchini), cucumbers, melons and watermelons. It is also found on the leaves of rose bushes, on vine leaves and on the tender shoots of peach and nectarine trees.

It can be controlled by spraying with sulphur or powdered algae, but this can also destroy beneficial fungi, making diluted milk or whey the preferred option (see page 153). To control powdery mildew in courgette plants it is enough just to remove old leaves, which is where the mildew develops.

Downy mildew This is a disease produced by fungi that appear as a greasy, ash-coloured powder on the face of the leaves. It asphyxiates the leaves and ends up drying them out. High ambient humidity produces favourable conditions for mildew, as does watering by sprinklers or persistent rain combined with temperatures of between 10° and 20°C/50° and 68°F. Mildew is easily spread by brushing against it or from wounds in the leaves. For this reason it is best neither to handle sensitive plants (tomatoes, vines, etc.) nor to touch the leaves when damp. In regions with a lot of rain or ambient humidity seek out varieties that are more resistant to fungal diseases.

In serious cases of mildew it is common to resort to copper-based solutions (oxychloride or copper sulphate and Bordeaux mixture). However, these can be toxic for the plants and the beneficial fungi in the earth. Instead of resorting to copper-based solutions, try preventative treatments made using decoctions of horsetail (*Equisetum arvense*), either alone or, more effectively, in conjunction with nettle tea. Milk whey solutions can also be used as a palliative measure (see page 153).

Rust This is produced by infestations of various fungi when the weather is humid and the vegetation is tender and exuberant. It appears as orange, yellow or brown spots. The best way to prevent it is to ensure that there is good air circulation around the plants.

Botrytis or grey mould This produces putrefaction and grey downy patches in the areas infested. The plant tissue loses its colour, deteriorates and dies. Cut out infected parts and prune back surplus foliage to aerate the plant. Botrytis can be treated with horsetail, milk whey or propolis tincture.

Mediterranean fruit fly

Commonly known as medfly, this is perhaps one of the most problematic pests in the Mediterranean. It lays its eggs inside fresh fruit – such as apricots, plums, peaches, nectarines and oranges – just before the fruit starts ripening and turns it maggotty. After all the care you have lavished on the plant you are likely to be left fruitless. The few biological control options available involve hanging pheromone traps (only effective over large areas) and protecting each fruit in a bag. You can also hang containers half filled with diluted fruit juice from the tree, but this has the disadvantage of attracting beneficial insects as well.

Moles

To get rid of moles you can try using smoke or strong smells. Another method is to hang empty glass bottles from iron rods stuck in the ground next to molehills. When the wind blows the bottles bang against the rods, making sounds and vibrations that bother the moles so that they go in search of quieter areas. Pushing bits of thorny bramble down the hole is also said to cause them to seek out pleasanter homes.

Nematodes

These are microscopic worms that live in the soil and as parasites on roots that then produce swellings and tumours. A very effective way of dealing with an infestation is to sow French marigolds (*Tagetes patula*). The flowers' roots exude a substance that inhibits the nematodes' development. Other plants with a repelling effect are *Schkuhria seneciodes*, *Helenium* and *Gallardia*. Another option is covering the ground with thick black plastic. This reduces the nematode population considerably, while having very little effect on the beneficial micro-organisms in the soil. There are also many fungi in the soil and in compost that are parasites on the nematodes and normally prevent them from proliferating. Thus the use of

Powdery mildew.

Downy mildew.

APPENDICES

fungicides, which also destroys these useful colonies of fungi, only aggravates the problem.

Potato beetle
This is one of the pests that most preoccupies gardeners and attacks both potatoes and aubergines. However, in organic agriculture it is rare to have a serious attack.

If you have only a few potato or aubergine plants manual control is probably easiest. Lift up the leaves and look for nests of eggs on the underside (recognizable as yellow patches). To get rid of them, either squash them or tear off the bit of leaf they are on.

In a case of serious attack you can resort to the use of *Bacillus thuringiensis* ('Karkovsky' variety), which is very effective when used during the larval phase of the potato beetle. Apply it in the evening, as strong sunlight degrades the bacteria and it loses effect.

Slugs and snails
The most intelligent approach is perhaps to encourage the presence of their predators, such as hedgehogs, toads or ducks. Failing that, the most nature-friendly way is to pick them off manually, taking advantage of a rainy day, when slugs and snails come out. Distributing old tiles or other forms of shelter around the garden under which snails will gather makes collection easier. Barriers, whether of ash, sawdust, copper sulphate or other substances, do not tend to work, as they are rapidly washed away by rain or dew. Some gardeners recommend eggshells broken up during a waning moon and spread around the plants on a waxing moon. Caffeine is a proven repellent and kills snails at higher concentrations. For a repellent effect, water plants and the ground or mulched ground around them with a watering can filled with 1 part strong coffee to 20 parts water. Increasing the concentration of coffee to 1 to 10 makes it lethal for snails.

An interesting way to deal with the problem is to get hold of some ducks and leave them to stroll around the garden from time to time. They are great devourers of slugs and snails but should not be left to wander at all times in the garden, as once they have finished with the snails they tend to take a liking to fresh greens, to devastating effect.

Another solution is to use beer. Slugs' fondness for beer is well known. Bury recycled containers with some 2cm/¾in of beer at ground level. The slugs and occasional snail that come to drink the beer end up drowning in it. The containers need to be emptied and refilled every two or three days. Experience shows that slugs prefer some brands to others. On the same night thirty slugs were found in a container containing one type of beer whereas in the container next to it, filled with a different brand, there was not a single one.

In very difficult cases of slug or snail infestation you can use iron phosphate granules, spreading them at a rate of one granule every 3cm/1¼in.

In specialized shops you can buy cultures of certain nematodes that feed on slugs are slug parasites. These, when spread around the garden, keep down the slug population.

Damage caused by a potato beetle.

Traps filled with beer can help control slugs.

Snails are best removed manually.

151

The southern green shield bug is a sap-sucking pest.

Southern green shield bugs

Unlike the innocuous green shield bug native to Britain, the southern green shield bug can be a serious pest, especially towards the end of the summer. By means of an oral stylus it sucks the sap from the tissue of plants, at the same time injecting necrosis-producing toxins and enzymes into the tissue. It can also be a vector of pathogenic fungi and in some gardens its presence in large numbers can have a very negative effect on plants' development, on the harvest and on the quality of the seed and its future germinating power.

In small gardens the bugs can be picked off by hand. Even so they may continue arriving; damage caused can be seen in the yellowing, deformation and drying out of leaves and fruit. The bugs are resistant and difficult to control using environment friendly pesticides such as neem or pyrethrum. Apart from trying to grow healthy plants, you can use preventative treatments. Decoctions of wormwood or tansy together with insect repellents made from garlic extract, chilli peppers and onions can be alternated with spraying potassium soap.

Spider mites (red or orange or yellow)

These are tiny reddish or yellow spiders about 5mm across that live on the underside of leaves. The typical patches formed by their colonies yellow the leaves and finally cause them to dry up. They generally appear in periods of water stress, such as droughts or when watering has been insufficient. When the soil is very dry it produces hot vapours, providing the perfect environment for most types of mite. Thus it is important to keep the ground damp and perhaps to water by sprinkler plants that are susceptible to red spider mite, such as green beans. It is advisable, as with aphids, to limit the amount of nitrogen that crops receive. In really bad cases you might resort to using pressurized water sprays on the undersides of the plant's bottom leaves. Slaked lime mixed with wood ash and left to stand tends to be very effective against mites. Spraying crops with infusions or decoctions of wormwood, nettles or horsetail also gives good results. Pyrethrum or neem can be used as a last resort.

Viruses

If you investigate the subject of viruses you will find that in nature, inside plants and animals there are thousands of endogenous viruses that live in positive synergy. Among these are some that in unfavourable conditions can cause problems for plant growth. Problematic viruses usually affect a plant by stunting its growth or turning leaves yellow and mottled. The surest way to avoid virus problems is to change the plant varieties you grow for ones that are more resistant to viruses. The use of some medicinal plant essences mitigates the effect of the viruses, as does garlic extract and propolis. The biodynamic preparation made with cow dung revitalizes the soil and the plants, curbing the negative effects of certain viruses.

Whitefly

Whitefly flourishes in humid environments. It sucks the sap of plants and secretes a sticky substance. A parasitic wasp, *Encarsia formosa*, is used to control it. Treating affected plants with a solution of 1 per cent potassium soap generally gives good results. In the case of a massive attack that proves resistant to soap you can resort to applying water vapour to the underside of the leaves, where whitefly tends to lodge. As a last resort plant-based insecticides such as pyrethrum or neem can be used.

Woodlice

There are many varieties of woodlice; the most common have a flattened shape and a grey-brown shell, while others are covered in a white down. They feed on sap and excrete a sticky treacle-like substance that ends up covering the leaves. This provides a base on which black sooty mould grows, leaving the infested leaves dirty and black. An Australian butterfly is commonly used as a predator in biological forms of control. Also effective are washing leaves with a pressurized water spray and treatment with potassium soap and plant-based insecticides.

Controlling problems caused by fungi

Encouraging biodiversity is perhaps the most effective way to avoid problems with parasitic fungi. For this reason it is important not to use fungicides that can damage useful fungi (the fungus *Trichoderma harzianum*, for example, is useful in getting rid of problematic fungi such as sclerotinia, to which it is antagonistic).

Aeration and pruning Fungal diseases or moulds often occur in plants that need their foliage to be dry. Lack of aeration, sun, watering by sprinklers or overly dense foliage can all cause humidity. Pruning and clearing around plants can improve aeration. However, if the problem persists it is best to move plants to a different site or choose a variety that is more resistant to fungal diseases.

Copper Stick a bit of copper wire in the stalk of affected plants (especially tomatoes) and twist it around the stalk in a spiral. Through osmosis the copper ions will circulate through the plant by means of the sap. This makes it difficult for mildews and moulds to develop, thus protecting the plant.

Milk whey Milk, and especially milk whey or yoghurt, has been shown to protect plants from parasitic fungi and has proven fungicidal effects on mildew.

The most effective solution is 1 part milk whey or yoghurt to 20 parts water or, if using milk, whole or skimmed, 1 part milk to 10 of water. It appears that the active ingredient is lactic acid, so the liquid from sauerkraut should also work.

Dusting or spraying Copper-based fungicides such as Bordeaux mixture are not always accepted in organic gardening and should only ever be used as a last resort. The copper salts that control the attack also have an effect on the mycorrhizae on which plants depend for their nutrition, as well as on other fungi that are antagonistic to the pathogens and might help prevent future plagues. Spraying with decoctions of horsetail or milk whey solutions, on the other hand, gives good results against pathogenic fungi without having any effect on the mycorrhizae.

When to resort to plant treatments

It should be emphasized that before resorting to any treatment first try to detect the cause and any mistakes you have made. Then, at the same time as any treatment, aim to increase the overall health of the plants. See to their basic needs, respect their biological cycles and rotations, choose varieties adapted to the area and pay special attention to the soil, ensuring its correct structure and as far as possible its microbial life.

Applications of plant extracts can be used preventatively, as reinforcing treatments, for their stimulating properties or as foliar fertilizers. Ideally they should be applied every ten to fifteen days; applying them more frequently (e.g. every two or three days) is not only unnecessary but can also provoke imbalances in the levels of enzymes and bacteria.

Only in cases of persistent pest attack (for instance, of aphids or whitefly) or in periods when fungal attack is likely is it a good idea to apply treatments weekly. For fruit trees, treating them once a season or every month or two may be enough.

The key is to use plant extracts as nutrient providers and reinforcing treatments for plants, and to maintain plant health and vitality with a healthy, fertile, humus-rich soil, adequate watering and the right conditions of sunlight and air for each crop.

In principle there is not much sense in making treatments 'just in case' and you should only intervene when faced with clear imbalances. The best way to practise organic gardening is to do everything possible to maintain the equilibrium in the garden at all times.

In the normal course of things plant preparations can be used when crops are in a delicate or stressful phase such as sowing, pricking out, transplanting, grafting, branch or tip pruning.

How to make plant preparations

Maceration, fermentations and slurries Leave cut-up fresh plants in water at the ambient temperature to dilute their active properties (1kg/2.2lb of plants to 10 litres/2½ gallons of water). The time they are left to macerate determines the process. Leaving them in water for twenty-four hours produces a maceration, two or three days a fermentation and more than three days a slurry. The most effective and classic macerations are those of nettle (commonly known as nettle tea), radish and nasturtium, which have stimulating, repellent,

reinforcing and nutritional effects. You can increase their scope, making them, for example, insecticidal by adding potassium soap or fungicidal by adding milk whey at the moment of application (½ litre of whey for every 1 litre of water in which plants have macerated).

Infusions Pouring boiling water over the plants (especially the tender leaves) and leaving them to macerate for five to ten minutes transfers the therapeutic, active constituents to water faster than fermenting or tinctures. A nettle infusion has insecticide and anti-aphid effects and some farmers have found that applying it hot (45–50°C/113–122°F) is more effective and does no damage to plants.

Decoctions Simmer the medicinal plants in a covered sau – cepan for ten to thirty minutes and leave them to settle for half an hour before filtering. This transfers most of the minerals and active plant-protecting constituents to the water, with the exception of vitamins and antioxidants that degrade in heat. Leave the decoction to cool down with the plants still in it to get a stronger solution. Examples of decoctions are that of horsetail, which is used as a fungicide, and that of comfrey, which is used as a leaf fertilizer, insecticide and mild fungicide.

Tinctures Macerating plants in alcohol transfers the active constituents contained in the plant more rapidly than macerating them in water. Eight hours in alcohol is enough to make a tincture and eight days is the maximum plants should be left in the alcohol. The tincture should be filtered and kept in a cool, dark place. The tincture concentrates many active constituents and has the advantage that it can be kept for months. The insecticide effects of garlic and tomato shoot tincture are well known.

Some plant treatments

Garlic Garlic is used as a repellent and general insecticide and also has fungicidal effects. It can be used to protect plants sensitive to fungal attack (such as mildew) and to deter aphids and mites. Garlic also repels potato beetle. The active acids in garlic penetrate the treated plants and circulate via the sap, thus getting to all parts of the plant and exercising a repelling effect. The acids also have regenerative, antiseptic and virucidal effects. Garlic tincture can be made by leaving cut-up garlic cloves in alcohol (20 per cent by volume) to macerate for eight days. Apply diluted in water, using 10–20ml of tincture per litre of water. Garlic can also be macerated in vegetable oil but needs three weeks before it is ready. The easiest and most practical method is to use garlic cut up and diluted in water and filtered, or liquidized. Use 1 head of garlic per 10 litres/2 ½ gallons of water.

In case of attack by mildew, aphids or mites make preventative treatments every three days or once a week.

Wormwood Macerated in water or as a decoction, wormwood has a repellent effect on ants, caterpillars, slugs, aphids and some types of mite. Use 300g/11oz of fresh wormwood per litre/32 fl oz of water. A wormwood decoction applied to apple and pear trees repels codling moth from laying its eggs in the fruit and turning it wormy.

Horsetail Decoction of horsetail (*Equisetum arvense*) provides good preventative treatment against fungal attack and also reinforces and provides minerals to plants because of its silica

153

content. Use 1kg/2.2lb of fresh plant for every 10 litres/2½ gallons of water. Applied in conjunction with fermented nettle extract, it is very effective against fungal diseases such as powdery mildew, downy mildew, rust, etc. It is also effective against aphids and red spider mite.

Comfrey Comfrey is very rich in potassium. Fermentations of comfrey repel fruit flies and moths from laying eggs in fruit trees. Adding comfrey leaves to compost heaps increases the level of minerals, especially potassium, in the compost.

Nettle Nettle strengthens plants against aphids and woolly apple aphids, and stimulates growth in young plants. Leave 1kg/2.2lb of fresh nettles in 10 litres/2½ gallons of water to ferment for two or three days. Once fermented, it should be filtered and every litre/16 fl oz diluted in 10–20 litres/2½–5 gallons of water. Undiluted, it can be used to stimulate the composting process.

Pyrethrum anacyclus A member of the daisy family, this has flowers that have a strong insecticide effect while having few effects on warm-blooded animals. It can be grown in the garden and the crushed-up flower heads put in jars of seeds (such as green beans and peas) to prevent weevil attack. Boiling up the flower buds (10g /0.4oz per litre/34 fl oz of water) supplies a natural wide-spectrum insecticide. It should only be applied at dusk, as it degrades rapidly in the sun.

Castor oil plant The plants and its seeds are highly toxic. In Bolivia the cut-up seeds of castor oil plant are put in the dry gourds in which seeds are kept to protect against weevils and other parasites.

Tobacco The nicotine present in the tobacco plant is toxic, making it a potent insecticide. Traditionally farmers grew a few tobacco plants in their garden and made a decoction from the leaves for use as an insecticide. Nicotine is not permitted in organic agriculture but gardeners not selling their produce commercially sometimes grow a few plants to use in emergency.

Thyme The oil present in thyme reinforces plants' vitality and is a repellent with a mild insecticide effect on aphids and mites.

Valerian Valerian generally increases plant resistance and improves soil life. Use 1 drop of extract per litre/34 fl oz of water.

Safer pesticides and treatments

When there is no other option but direct attack on your plants' aggressors, there is a wide range of possibilities from plant extracts and plant-based insecticides that are non-toxic for humans to products such as potassium soap or clay. Natural neem or pyrethrum-based insecticides can be bought commercially. In the specific case of types of worm, caterpillars or any moth or butterfly larva, *Bacillus thuringiensis* can be used.

However, in practice for most garden pests and plant diseases there are ingenious ecological solutions that make even the use of natural insecticides unnecessary. As the Spanish gardener Jesus Arnau writes, 'When a plague appears we tend to ask the wrong question: "What should I do about this plague?" we ask, instead of "Why has this plague appeared?" If we do not change the question, we will never understand anything. It is as though we are not willing to look, as when we go to the doctor hoping to be prescribed a

magic pill and are not happy to be told we should change our diet or give up smoking. When we rush to use an insecticide, albeit a natural one, we are only changing the conventional magic pill for the ecological one.'

Before using any treatment you need to analyse the possible causes for the plague, including taking stock of any mistakes you might have made. In parallel to applying any treatment you should boost the plants' general health, seeing to their basic needs, respecting rotations and biological cycles, choosing varieties adapted to the local conditions and paying special attention to the soil in which plants grow, improving its structure and microbiotic life as far as possible.

Pyrethrum This contains plant extracts rich in natural pyrethrins that have a strong insecticide effect on most plant pests, such as mites, aphids, white fly, thrips, red spider mite, potato beetle, flea beetles, leek moth, bed bugs and ants. Dilute according to manufacturers' instructions and apply in the evening, as it degrades in sunlight. In cases of serious attack treatment can be repeated after two days and a third treatment made a week or ten days later. You should not make a habit of reaching for treatments containing pyrethrins; nor should they be used 'just in case'. These are wide-spectrum insecticides and their toxicity (they attack the nervous system) has negative effects on fauna, fish and earthworms. Avoid the use of pyrethroids (synthetic forms of pyrethrins) and insecticides that mix natural pyrethrins with synthetic chemical insecticides.

Potassium soap This works by diluting the waxy layer that protects some insects (aphids, whitefly, thrips and woodlice) from dehydration. Dilute 1 per cent soap in water for whitefly and 2 per cent for aphids, thrips and woodlice. Before applying in big amounts do tests to work out different plants' tolerance to the product.

Bacillus thuringiensis These are bacteria that produce toxic crystalline proteins that paralyze the digestive system of most moth and butterfly larvae without risk to humans or the environment. Apply at dusk, as sunlight destroys the bacteria, and make regular treatments, as it degrades easily.

Neem The neem tree is originally from Asia. Its seeds are used to make an insecticide, the use of which is authorized in organic agriculture, as it is non-toxic for humans and warm-blooded animals. It is effective against a wide variety of insects and also used to get rid of parasites in domestic and farm animals. It is present in different preparations, and the proportion used and how depends on the extract used. The most common method is to dilute neem extract or oil in water and apply it as a spray.

Biofumigation This consists in letting weeds grow, cutting them down and digging them into the soil. The ground is then covered with transparent or black plastic to heat it up. The heat causes the plants inside to ferment, generating substances toxic to soil pathogens and naturally disinfecting the soil.

Sodium bicarbonate This is used as a fungicide. Dilute 1 spoonful of sodium bicarbonate in 1 litre /34 fl oz of water.

Milk It has been proven that milk, milk whey or yoghurt diluted with water has much the same fungicidal and anti-mildew effects as chemical fungicides – see page 153.

Clay Daubing tree trunks with a mixture of clay, horsetail decoction and some powdered silica heals wounds in the bark and fights canker.

Cold water, pressurized water and water vapour Cold pressurized water has the same effect as a strong rain in cleaning plants of plagues of pests. Keeping the surface of the ground always damp can be enough to avoid problems with mites, and wetting the underside of leaves well gives good results. Water vapour is applied most effectively by a domestic steam-cleaning machine, as this dissolves insects' waxy protective cover with greater ease. There is no need to fear using vapour, as plants have a system for rapidly dissipating excessive heat when it is not prolonged. In any case, you can test plants' resistance to it.

Foliar feeds These can be made from well-diluted liquid algae extracts, milk whey or mature compost. Use rainwater to make the dilutions and spray on to leaves.

Sulphur Dusting with sulphur has been widely used to prevent mildew and fungal attack on the leaves of tomatoes and cucurbits (courgettes, melons, cucumbers, etc.) and for the control of red spider mite in green beans and tomatoes. It can increase soil acidity and in high doses or repeated applications it can inhibit beneficial mycorrhizae in the soil. Apply at dusk or early morning, never in full sun or when temperatures are high.

Oils Shop-bought mineral or rapeseed oils can be used in winter to control aphids and woodlice in fruit trees.

Ashes Wood ash recently taken from a stove or bonfire is caustic. Some gardeners sprinkle it on aphid colonies or on soil where there are flea beetles or slugs. It is common to sprinkle ash in a circle around recently transplanted cabbages and lettuces.

Plant essential oils Essential oils extracted by distillation from medicinal plants such as lavender, mint or thyme can be used to stimulate and reinforce plants, and also to repel insects. Preparations consisting of a mix of essential oils for use in organic gardening are available commercially.

Propolis This is made by bees and is a mixture of waxes, tree resins and the active protective substances that cover all plant shoots. It has fungicidal, insecticidal and even virucidal properties. It is a scarce and therefore expensive product, but only very little is needed. You can buy tinctures and extracts or make your own using propolis from your own beehives or bought directly from beekeepers. The tincture is very concentrated and only 15 to 50 drops of tincture for 1 litre/34 fl oz of water are needed. Propolis can be used in combination with other treatments or medicinal plant preparations, thus reinforcing their preventative and curative effect.

INDEX

Numbers in **bold** refer to main entries, numbers in *italic* to illustrations.

PHOTOGRAPHIC ACKNOWLEDGMENTS

All photographs copyright © Mariano Bueno except for the following:
© Chris Caldicott pages 10, 54-5, 82-3;
© Jean-François Dessup page 121; © Dmitry page 119 (above); © Dolnikov page 94 (right); © Emer page 127 (left); by Niccoló Grassi © Frances Lincoln Ltd pages 118, 126; © Gudmund page 119 (below); © Conny Hagen page 133; © Herculaneum 79 page 95 (right); by Echter Kümmel © Sunday Pictures page 91 (left); © Mary Lane page 132; © Eduardo Mencos pages 9, 102-3, 132-5; © Maddeline Monroe page 90 (right); © Johanna Mühlbauer page 106; © Gillian Paire page 124; © Pefkos page 92 (right); © Norman Pogson page 122; © Anette Linnea Rasmussen page 129; © Yves Roland page 117; © Tom Sturm page 112; © Stuart Taylor page 115; © Steven Wooster pages 2-3; © Xiaodong Ye page 127 (right).